ALTERNATIVE HEALTH

HERBAL MEDICINE

ANNE McINTYRE

ILLUSTRATED BY SHAUN WILLIAMS

Charles E. Tuttle Company, Inc.
Boston • Rutland, Vermont • Tokyo

HERBAL MEDICINE

First published in the United States of America by
Charles E. Tuttle Company, Inc.
of Rutland, Vermont, and Tokyo, Japan, with editorial offices at
77 Central Street, Boston, Massachusetts 02109

ISBN 0-8048-1837-1

Cover art by Isabella Groblewski
Cover design by Fahrenheit

First Printing 1993

Printed in the United States of America

HERBAL MEDICINE

CONTENTS

INTRODUCTION

We are witnessing an enormous revival of interest in herbal medicine. Thirty years ago a re-emergence of this ancient art of healing would have been difficult to imagine. It appeared to be on the brink of extinction, while the public put their faith in the wonder drugs of medical science such as penicillin and cortisone.

Since then, the unforeseen side-effects of many drugs and the sometimes even tragic consequences of taking them have made people increasingly aware of the risks that accompany modern medication. In addition, a large number of illnesses have failed to respond to drug treatment, and patients' hopes of a wonder cure have been dashed. People are coming to realize that the 'magic bullets' do not hold all the answers to chronic degenerative diseases such as rheumatism and arthritis, nor to stress-related illness.

Instead of relying entirely on the authoritarian figure of the doctor and unquestioningly swallowing the drugs the chemist doles out, people are beginning to want to take more responsibility for their own health. They want medical treatment that is safe and gentle, and they want to be able to participate in their own cure. This means seeking natural therapy.

In a more general sense, people are beginning to question what they are putting into their bodies and how it affects their health, and this includes not only drugs, but also foods, the water we drink and the air we breathe. 'Natural' has become synonymous with good, wholesome and healthy. This new awareness has been reflected throughout the consumer world, and almost every town now has its own health food shop. The demand for pure, uncontaminated produce has spread to the supermarkets, which are responding by providing wholefoods and organically grown vegetables. Hundreds of books have appeared, extolling the virtues of natural foods and explaining the importance of vitamins and minerals.

Along with this concern with health and all things natural have mushroomed many different natural therapies, some ancient and for many years neglected and forgotten, others new and fashionable. The range of therapies offered is wide, and it can be difficult deciding which therapy best suits a particular case, and how to tell a therapist to be trusted from a quack simply jumping on the bandwagon.

People have had faith in herbs for thousands of years. We all consume herbs in some form or other, even if it is only a sprig of parsley in a salad or the tang of peppermint in toothpaste. The culinary use of herbs forms an accepted part of the cook's tradition — lamb and mint sauce, sage and onion stuffing, and fish garnished with dill.

The renewed interest in all things natural has meant

THE HERBAL PILLOW — ONE OF MANY REFLECTIONS OF OUR INCREASING INTEREST IN NATURE ...

that more people are using herbs in wider aspects of their lives. People are buying herbal cosmetics, face creams, shampoos and body lotions — the herbal ingredients supply a promise of healthier hair and skin synonymous with beauty. The shelves of health food shops are loaded with herbal remedies for almost every ailment. People are drinking herbal teas, sleeping on herb pillows and using herbal potions for their pets. Any bookshop or library with an alternative medicine section will stock more books on herbs and their uses than on any other subject.

But there is little or no information about the practice of herbal medicine today. People need to know how to relate what they read about the healing properties of herbs to themselves. They need to know what to expect if they consult a medical herbalist about their health. Many people are not even aware that there is such a person as a medical herbalist to help them.

The overall impression to be gained from current literature and advertising is that herbal medicine belongs to the simple country life of our ancestors, when people lived on the land and grew their own food and herbs. The image is endearing, but does not present a clear picture of herbal medicine as it is practised now.

This book aims to offer a clear representation of the practice of modern herbal medicine. Herbalism is a system of medicine in its own right, offering treatment for a wide variety of illnesses. Herbalists can be found in clinics in most areas, treating even the most serious diseases with herbs which have been tested by time and proved to be not only gentle and effective, but also without the risk of toxic side-effects.

1.
WHAT IS HERBAL MEDICINE?

Herbal medicine is the treatment of disease using medicinal plants, both internally and externally, to restore the patient to health. It is a system of medicine that relies on the therapeutic qualities of plants to help the patient by enhancing the body's own recuperative powers. It is a natural method of healing based on the traditional usage of herbs coupled with modern scientific developments.

The word 'herb' generally brings to mind the dried leaves of seasoning plants used in cooking, such as rosemary or sage. In a medical context herbs are any plants, including flowers or trees, which possess curative properties.

A BRIEF HISTORY OF HERBALISM

Ancient origins

Herbal medicine is as old as human life. Along with other therapies such as osteopathy, acupuncture, chiropractic and homoeopathy, it is often referred to as 'alternative' medicine. However, it may be more appropriate to say that herbal medicine is not the alternative, but the original medicine. It is not a new invention, but an ancient tradition.

In the Bible, Genesis 1, v. 28-30, it says,

And God said, I have given you every herb bearing seed,

which is upon the face of the earth, and every tree, in which is the fruit of a tree yielding seed: to you it shall be meat. And to every beast of the earth and to every fowl of the air and to everything that creepeth upon the earth, wherein is life, I have given green herb for meat, and it was so.

And in Psalms 104, v. 14, it says,

He caused the grass to grow for cattle, and the herb for the service of man ...

Herbal medicine is not a fashionable therapy that has sprung up in response to the great demand for natural therapeutics. The origins of herbal medicine are lost in the mists of time and certainly predate all existing records.

How humans discovered herbs

Ever since the dawn of life we have been using the herbs around us to treat our health problems. As a dog will eat couch grass as an emetic or to aid digestion, so our ancestors' instincts led them to discover the right astringent fruits and leaves to cure diarrhoea, the right leaves or flowers for colic. A story is told about a muskrat which was seen to injure itself jumping over a fence. It climbed up a pine tree, covering its wounds with the resin, and then sat alternately in the sunshine and shade to speed the process of recovery. Female deer know that eating the leaves of the martagon lily puts them on heat. A wolf that has been bitten by a snake will dig up and eat the roots of bistort, which purges it of the toxin.

Doctrine of signatures

Perhaps we discovered our remedies by a system of trial and error, rather than by instinctive knowledge. We can only guess. Ancient herbalists believed that the Creator had provided relief from every disease, and for guidance to humankind had imprinted on each herb certain signs. This vegetable language was called the 'doctrine of signatures'.

HEARTSEASE THE NAME GIVEN TO THE WILD PANSY, IS SAID TO EASE THE PAIN OF SEPARATION FROM A LOVED ONE. THE FLOWER RESEMBLES THE SHAPE OF THE HUMAN HEART.

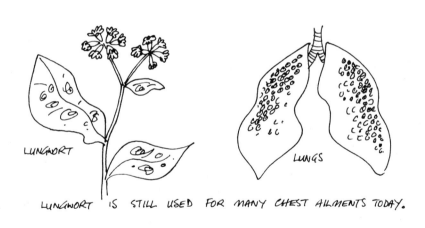

LUNGWORT IS STILL USED FOR MANY CHEST AILMENTS TODAY.

CAMOMILE HAS A HISTORY OF USE AS AN EYE REMEDY.

One of the best known examples of the doctrine was the red beet with its branching red veins through the green leaf signifying a cure for heart and circulation problems. The form of the red beetroot corresponds to the shape of the heart, and the veins in the leaf branch as ours do. Similarly, lungwort has speckled leaves which were said to resemble the shape and pattern of the lungs, and the plant is still used today for lung problems. Many of the remedies used for the liver are yellowish. Yellow is the colour of bile, a secretion associated with the function of the liver, and the colour of jaundice, an illness associated with its malfunction. The yellow of the remedy comes from the root of the plant, in the case of the yellow dock, or from the juice, as with the greater celandine. Pilewort or lesser celandine has root tubers that rather resemble haemorrhoids, and is used to treat them.

However we may have discovered our remedies, a wealth of herbal knowledge gradually grew up over the centuries. Tested by time, it was transmitted from one generation to the next. This knowledge was common to all cultures throughout the world — it is interesting to note that today herbal medicine is still the main form of medical treatment, among 85 per cent of the world's population.

Written records
The earliest records of herbal medicine are the Chinese treatises attributed to the Yellow Emperor around 2500 BC, called the Pen T'sao. The Ebers Papyrus of 1500 BC contains references to more than 700 herbal remedies, many of which are still used in modern herbalism. Records prove that several other nations, notably the Persians, Indians and Aztecs, possessed knowledge of plants for medicinal use well over a thousand years before the birth of Christ.

The Greeks and Romans, especially Hippocrates, who is traditionally regarded as the Father of Medicine, Dioscoides and Theophrastus, furthered the knowledge of herbal medicine. Claudius Galen, born in AD 130, wrote the famous Greek herbal *De Simplicibus,* which, along with other Greek herbals, was used and added to by herbalists throughout the Dark Ages.

Handwritten copies of old manuscripts by Theophrastus, Dioscoides and Pliny survived into the Middle Ages and came into universal reading with the introduction of the printing press. New medical books were also among those first printed, including *The Leech Book of Bald.* Gerarde, the herbalist to James I, had a garden in Holborn containing over 1,000 varieties of herbs, and in his *Herbal* of 1597, he tells of medicinal herbs growing in the marshes at Paddington and in the ditches of Piccadilly. In 1649 the famous Nicolas Culpeper wrote his *English Physician* and *Physical Dictionary.*

Herbalism in decline
In the 16th century herbalism was still the dominant form of healing. But Paracelsus (1493-1541) had already laid the foundation for the use of chemical compounds in medicine. He introduced iron, antimony, mercury and other inorganic substances into medical practice, and physicians rapidly began to forsake the safety of botanical remedies for the use of minerals in large and dangerous doses. Herbal medicine thus gradually fell from prominence, although it was still practised by many humble people in their own homes.

Herbalism in America
As herbalism was going into decline in Europe, it was being developed in America. Some of the Pilgrim Fathers who made their way across the Atlantic in the *Mayflower* were well versed in herblore, and they joined their knowledge to that of the Native Americans, who had been using herbal medicine for centuries. It was not long before the settlers had adopted native remedies from plants such as black and blue cohosh, squaw vine, false unicorn root and golden seal. These are still favourites among herbalists today.

A descendant of one of the Pilgrim Fathers, Samuel

Thomson (1769-1843), is famous for popularizing an ancient Native American lobelia remedy, and for establishing herbal schools and botanic societies all over the United States. In 1830 Dr A.I. Coffin brought Thomson's system of medicine to Europe, and thus the wheel turned full circle. Coffin did much to revive herbal medicine in Britain by lecturing and writing about it. In 1864 he was instrumental in bringing together a number of eminent herbalists to form the National Association of Medical Herbalists, now renamed the National Institute of Medical Herbalists (NIMH).

The analytical eye of chemistry
The first half of the 19th century saw a resurgence of interest in herbal medicine, but the second half witnessed a further decline. For it was at this time that the infant but rapidly progressing science of chemistry focused its analytical eye on medicinal herbs, and made them one of its main spheres of interest.

In time chemists succeeded in isolating the therapeutically active substances from medicinal plants. For example, in 1827, they isolated the glycoside salicin from willow bark. It forms the basis of the well-known drug aspirin.

In many instances the use of these isolated active substances began to replace the use of the whole plant.

Then came the first synthetic drugs: anaesthetics, followed by antiseptics. In 1874 sodium salicylate, which acts like aspirin, was first synthesized in a laboratory. Herbal remedies were becoming obsolete. For almost a century, they continued to be pushed into the background while synthetic medicines increased in number and complexity. Only recently have herbal remedies begun to regain popularity and find a significant place in modern medical care.

Gradually it is being realized that the use of isolated active substances, whether natural or synthetic, is responsible for the array of side-effects which can accompany orthodox treatment. With reference to aspirin, it must have shaken the foundations of chemical medicine

THEY'll find a couple of teaspoons of this more agreeable than a visit from the sawbones, I'll warrant...

when, on 10 June 1986, all children's aspirin-based drugs were taken off the market, having been incriminated in the occurrence of Reye's Syndrome, which causes brain and kidney damage in children.

However, the chemical analysis of plants carried out in the 19th century has been of use to herbalism, because it laid the foundations of the pharmacological approach to herbal medicine. Since then the plant world has been explored extensively, and an increasing number of plants have been found to contain medicinal qualities. Chemical analysis of the ingredients of plants has proved scientifically the claims made by the ancient healers about their therapeutic powers. Herbal medicine may have its roots in 'magic', but is also validated by scientific fact.

The possibility of discovering further potent therapeutic agents in plants is immense and is now under investigation. Clues about which plants are likely to be suitable are often derived from the reputed action of the plant in folklore. For example, the Cancer Chemotherapy National Service Center in the USA has examined documents dating back to a few hundred years before the birth of Christ to find out what plants were used then in the treatment of malignant and non-malignant tumours. Thousands of plants are reputed to have anti-tumour activity, and as a result of recent investigation many of them have been pharmacologically analysed and their structures determined.

THE DIFFERENCE BETWEEN HERBAL AND CONVENTIONAL MEDICINE

Modern medicine's debt to herbs

Though there are those in the orthodox medical world who ignore herbal medicine, even condemn it as an anachronism, the constituents of herbs have provided the blueprint for many of the most effective and widely known drugs used today. 'Orthodox' medicine has its roots in herbal medicine.

Throughout history and in many parts of the world, plant discoveries have marked landmarks in medical progress. Ipecac is a South American plant which acts as an emetic to rid the body of poisons. It was once used throughout Europe to control bad cases of dysentery. Quinine comes from the bark of a South American tree, and has saved many thousands of people dying of malaria.

Rauwolfia root is a herbal remedy that has been used for centuries in African and India to treat 'moon madness'. It was brought to the attention of Western doctors when a Nigerian prince at a British university had a nervous breakdown and was finally treated by a tribal doctor with rauwolfia, which succeeded in curing him where conventional Western remedies had failed. Laboratory investigations on the plant isolated reserpine as the active constituent, and a breakthrough was made in the treatment of the mentally ill. Reserpine forms the basis of several anti-hypertensive drugs with sedative and tranquillizing effects.

Ma Huang *(Ephedra sinica)* is a plant that has been used by physicians in China for thousands of years. Chemists have extracted the alkaloid ephedrine from the plant, and this is used in medicine today for many purposes, including the relief of nasal congestion, bronchial coughs and asthma. However, ephedrine has been reported to raise blood pressure. In the whole plant used by the herbalist, there are six other alkaloids, the predominant one of which actually prevents the increase of blood pressure and heart rate. Thus the isolated drug can be rather dangerous, while the whole plant is balanced by nature in such a fashion as to make it a much safer remedy.

Another important drug was discovered in 1775 in an English country garden. William Withering, a Shropshire doctor, was concerned that there was no successful treatment for patients with heart problems. He more or less had to let them go home to die. To his great surprise, several of his patients with what he thought was terminal heart disease survived, and he discovered that they had been treated with a herbal remedy by an old lady nearby. She had a cure for dropsy — oedema, the disease where excess fluid accumulates in the body tissues because of a malfunction of the heart and/or kidneys.

Withering found that the predominant remedy the old lady used in her prescriptions was foxglove — digitalis. From then on he experimented ceaselessly with the plant and after years of work he managed to isolate the therapeutic agent, digoxin. Digitalis is well-known today as a medical heart remedy and digoxin is the agent used in chemical drugs.

Thus modern medicine is indebted to the plant world to a considerable degree. The scientific medical mind, however, rejects herbal remedies because of the impossibility of accurately measuring dosages. The ingredients of plants vary in strength according to the season, the day and even the hour. The laboratory has corrected these anomalies by first isolating and then synthesizing the plants' active principles. In this way chemists have overcome the inexactitudes of nature.

Using the whole plant

It is particularly the practice of isolating active principles from the whole plant that divides doctors from medical herbalists. Orthodox medicine is based on drugs isolated from plants, or more often manufactured in the laboratory. The herbalist advocates the use of the whole plant as a gentler and safer way of restoring a patient to health, and the herbalist's maxim therefore is: 'The whole plant is greater than the sum of its constituent parts.'

There are two different types of substances found in medicinal plants, and both have an important role to play in the healing process. The primary healing agents are the active ingredients which the early chemists were interested in extracting. The other compounds in the plant determine how effective the healing agent will be by making the body more or less receptive to its powers. Most healing plants contain several active substances, one of which will be dominant, and it is this one which influences the choice of plant by the herbal practitioner when making up a prescription for the patient.

However, the importance of the secondary healing agents should not be underestimated, because without them the active substances could have a totally different effect. It is the natural combination of both types of substance in the whole plant that puts the patient back on the road to health.

This point can be illustrated with the example of the herb meadowsweet. Meadowsweet contains as its active principle salicylic acid, and has an action which is similar to aspirin. It could be considered as the herbal equivalent of aspirin. It is widely known that aspirin can cause internal bleeding in people with sensitive stomach linings. Meadowsweet, on the other hand, is actually used by herbalists to treat an inflamed or bleeding stomach lining. Its secondary agents include tannin and mucilage, which act to protect and heal the mucous membrane of the stomach.

To illustrate this point further, most synthetic diuretics (drugs that increase the flow of urine) cause a loss of potassium from the body. Hence doctors need to prescribe a potassium supplement with diuretics to rectify the balance. Slow K is one such proprietary drug, and it can have the unfortunate side-effect of causing stomach ulceration in susceptible people. Herbalists use dandelion leaves as a diuretic. They have a high potassium content and so combine a non-toxic diuretic with an integral potassium supplement.

Herbalists do not agree with isolating and synthesizing active constituents and advocate instead the use of whole plant medicines to avoid harmful side-effects. Substances such as hormones, enzymes and trace elements, which accompany the active components in plants, ensure that these can be properly absorbed and assimilated.

Natural versus synthetic

Through their roots plants take up from the soil the minerals we need for health, transforming them into

materials that can easily be used by the human body.
Humans have always eaten plants, and so we have
adapted ourselves over millennia to respond to whole
plant medicines in a way that we cannot possibly respond
to powerful synthetic drugs.

The substances that plants contain are very similar in
chemical make-up to those that form our bodies. Medical
science believes that if the chemical formula of an
artificial product is similar to that of a natural one, it will
be assimilated as easily by the body. The herbalist does
not go along with this, and recognizes that drugs are
received by our systems as foreign substances that
increase the workload of that great detoxifying organ, the
liver, which must rid the body of the toxic materials
contained in the drug. Drugs are made from inert
substances, while plants are living organic materials.
Remedies based on chemicals will never compare
favourably with the fruits of nature.

Self-healing

Practitioners of herbal medicine believe in the inherent
power of the body to heal itself — the 'vital force' as it is
termed. Many in orthodox medicine think that patients
recover because of surgery or drugs alone and ignore the
presence of the vital force.

Herbalists recognize that there are forms of energy
which create and maintain life, and which can restore a
sick person to health. It has always been the aim of the
healer to activate these forces and not to treat the body as
an empty vessel devoid of life. Medicine is not just a
matter of chemistry alone. One of the maxims of natural
therapy is that medicine cannot change the workings of
the body, it can only help them. One of the oldest medical
teachings says, 'Medicus curat, natura sanat': 'The doctor
treats, but nature heals.'

Drugs or foods?

Herbal remedies act very much like foods; in fact many
common foods can be used for their medicinal actions:

IT HAS ALWAYS BEEN THE AIM OF THE HEALER NOT TO TREAT THE BODY AS AN EMPTY VESSEL DEVOID OF LIFE.

carrots are good for skin and urinary problems; oats are a wonderful tonic to the nervous system. We cannot assimilate directly many of the substances we need for building up and maintaining our health. Plants process these substances for us, making them accessible to the body. Herbs provide the body with minerals, vitamins and trace elements — the raw materials it needs for recovery. There are other medicinal substances in herbs which have affinities for particular organs and systems, and these act more specifically to promote the action of the body in its own efforts to heal.

Drugs are more direct and more dramatic in their action than herbs. They enter the blood stream more rapidly, their effects have a quicker onset, greater intensity and shorter duration. In many cases of acute and serious disease they can save lives, but nevertheless

25

they lower the general vitality of the body by increasing the work of elimination. In this way, rather than building up our general health, they diminish the strength of the body's own defence against disease.

Thus drugs will not necessarily help a person who has been worn down by chronic illness, or a person who is merely feeling 'under the weather'. Both cases, however, can benefit from treatment with herbal remedies. Herbs build up the body and gently nudge it back to health, never 'taking a hammer to crack a nut'.

Treating the whole person

A herbalist aims to establish the cause of the patient's problem through a lengthy consultation, and regards the patient as an entity. Treatment is aimed at the whole person — physical, emotional and mental.

In orthodox medicine, treatment is aimed at the physical part that has gone wrong; a remedy will be given, for example, to relax the bronchial tubes in asthma, with little consideration as to the cause of the disease, which could lie perhaps in the immune system in the form of an allergy, or in the nervous system, being related to emotional stress. Treating a limited aspect of the problem can amount to a straightforward suppression of the symptoms, instead of promoting the body's own healing powers, and adds to the accumulation of toxic waste in the body. While drug treatment can appear temporarily to improve health, it lowers the vitality of the patient, who is already under stress, and pushes the disease further into the body. This can actually lead to more serious and chronic disease later on in life as the body becomes less able to withstand the causes of disease it encounters daily.

A person treated with herbs may not necessarily recover as quickly as one treated with drugs, but once better the patient will feel stronger than after a course of orthodox medicine. By increasing general health and the efficiency of weak organs or systems, herbal medicine helps raise resistance to further illness and prevents chronic disease.

In summary
- Herbalists advocate the use of the whole plant, while orthodox medicine uses isolated or synthesized derivatives.
- Herbs are natural products which the body is accustomed to, while drugs are foreign substances which are treated as alien and toxic by the body, and can produce side-effects.
- Herbalists recognize the vital force and its efforts to heal the body, while orthodox medicine ignores it.
- Herbal remedies act like foods and build up the health of the body, providing it with the wherewithal to heal itself. Drugs have more dramatic and specific actions and decrease general health.
- Orthodox treatment is directed mainly towards the part of the body that is not functioning properly, and as such acts to suppress the symptoms of malfunction. Herbalists aim to treat the whole person and attempt to ascertain the causes of illness.
- Drugs act more quickly, while herbs can take longer to restore the patient to health. Drugs can act wonderfully in acute emergencies but often miss the point in more chronic disease where herbal medicine comes into its own.
- The two forms of medicine work differently but both are effective in their own way and will no doubt be used in the future to complement each other.

FOLKLORE, ART OR SCIENCE?

In the past many plants were considered special by those who knew of their valuable properties, and since people had little knowledge of how they effected such wonderful cures, they were associated with magic. It certainly is quite miraculous that a leaf or a flower or a root can treat illness, and it is not surprising that our ancestors glorified vegetable life because it sustained all other life — it provided them with food, medicine, shelter, clothing and fuel.

In our sophisticated times, we can stock our supermarkets and grocers' with every food that we need all the year round, but our forebears depended on the seasons for their sustenance. Not only that, but body, mind and spirit were elevated in the spring and perhaps dejected in the bleakness of winter. From this reliance on nature, the turning of the seasons, the regeneration of plant life in spring after the apparent death of winter, we developed an understandable awe and a great respect for nature, which we have largely lost today. It is easy to see why our ancestors attributed spiritual powers to plants in addition to their material ones.

Some of the extraordinary names of plants tell us much about the importance of plant life and how it was revered in the past. Plants that came into flower on St John's day, 24 June, were credited with healing powers acquired from St John himself. St John's wort has widely been considered a panacea for all ills. Other herb names such as blessed thistle, mother of millions, flesh and blood, tree of heaven, tree of life, blazing star, all-heal, self-heal and herb of grace reflect respect and gratitude for our God-given medicine chest.

To many, the idea of herbal medicine and herbalists conjures up the image of a wise old woman, living in a country cottage, mixing up strange brews in a dark kitchen over a blackened hob. In our scientific age such an image does not always inspire confidence.

Now, as a result of the work of pharmacognosists — pharmacologists specializing in natural remedies — medical herbalists are able to understand the scientific reasons for the workings of herbal medicines.

The work of the wise old woman has now been complemented by that of graduates from the school of herbal medicine, who have completed a long course, much of it devoted to conventional medical training in anatomy, physiology, pathology and diagnosis. They are well acquainted with the therapeutic effects of the herbs they prescribe, having studied their biochemistry and pharmacology.

Folklore has now been put under the microscope and hundreds of remedies which have been in use for centuries have been vindicated. Scientific explanations for the efficacy of herbal remedies are now being found through research as the many constituents of the plants are identified.

Aloe vera is a succulent reputed to have been used by Cleopatra. The University of Pennsylvania Radiology Department has found that the juice of this plant is more effective in treating radiation burns than any other known product. It is now one of the most popular herbs used commercially in face creams, hand and body lotions and shampoos.

The early Egyptians are also said to have eaten cabbage seed to prevent alcoholic intoxication. Dr William Shire, the American Chemical Society's biochemistry award winner, found that an amino acid in cabbage juice had excellent results in the treatment of alcoholism. In Germany sauerkraut juice is a popular pick-me-up for the 'morning after'.

Investigators at the Food and Drug Research Laboratories in Long Island, USA, analysed liquorice root

and found that it contains substances that are chemically similar to hormones from our adrenal cortex. It was proved to be useful in treating chronic skin conditions and healing gastric ulcers.

Many herbal remedies form the basis of modern orthodox medicines. The pharmaceutical industry harvests huge plantations of herbs for use in the production of drugs each year. It also grows herbs for further research activities. So, we have two sources of knowledge about the efficacy and also the safety of herbal medicines — ancient folklore and modern science. The empirical evidence gathered over thousands of years and proved by recent investigations means that patients may rest assured that the medicine of the herbalist is based on strong foundations.

Herbal medicine has a scientific basis, and healing — and the practice of herbalism — must always be an art, and requires skill. The whole person cannot be treated by science alone. Medical herbalists feel strongly that you cannot simply reduce a human being to the level of biochemistry. How otherwise could we explain human experiences of creativity and love, instinct and intuition,

religious inspiration and feelings of inner certainty?
Talking to the patient and taking a case history is an art,
as is making a clear diagnosis and establishing the causes
of ill-health.

To give an illustration, there is no one set of herbs for
the treatment of constipation. Before deciding which
treatment to prescribe, the herbalist must exercise
sensitivity assessing the nature of the patient. A tense and
jumpy person may be prone to muscle contraction. A
contracted bowel muscle could be the cause of
constipation. A patient who looks tired and 'sagging' lacks
muscular tone, and may well have flaccid, underactive
bowels. Observation of the patient can be confirmed by
physical examination. Herbs prescribed for the problem
are chosen to suit the case being treated, and are designed
to promote the action of the vital force accordingly. They
need to boost the body's own healing powers and not
interfere with them. Science tells us little of the vital force.
Modern herbalism is a marriage of art and science.

It is all too easy to underrate the power of herbs to heal,
and to dismiss those who practise the art of herbal
medicine as medical Rip Van Winkles, but nature is still
something we little understand despite our sophisticated
scientific discoveries. Thomas Edison once said, 'Until
man duplicates a blade of grass, Nature can laugh at his
so-called scientific knowledge.'

2.
HOW DOES HERBAL MEDICINE WORK?

THE PHILOSOPHY OF NATURAL HEALING

Natural healing is founded on the basic principle that the human organism possesses the inherent power to protect, regulate, adjust and heal itself. This power is the vital force, an energy which medical science tends by and large to ignore because it is intangible and immeasurable, and at present too subtle for scientific investigation.

However, Walter Cannon, Professor Emeritus of Physiology at Harvard Medical School, has conducted experiments and investigations into the nature of this healing force and has produced scientific evidence of its existence. He coined the word 'homoeostasis' for the steady state that we are able to maintain within our bodies despite the constant onslaught of powerful external influences which seek to upset our equilibrium. The poor food that we often eat, devitalized and full of chemicals, the alcohol and drugs we consume, the polluted air we breathe, overwork, tension and anxiety can all contribute to unbalance us.

Despite these adverse influences, the body daily gives us evidence of its powers of self-renewal. Take the simple and easily observed example of a minor cut or graze. As soon as the skin is broken, the body starts putting its healing process into operation, forming blood clots to prevent further bleeding, manufacturing fibrin to close the wound.

Unknown to most of us, the body is quietly performing other miraculous feats at the same time. White blood cells, anti-toxins and antibiotics are immediately rallied and rushed into concentration at the site of trauma, where they help to immobilize and destroy the bacteria that have entered the body through the wound. They also start to break down and dispose of the debris from the wound, including the dead bacteria. The cells in the area surrounding the wound that have escaped trauma and remain undamaged increase their workload by supplying extra oxygen, food and materials for repairing the damaged tissues and building new ones. Even a simple cut actually involves a very complex process necessitating co-ordinated activity from several of the body's systems. Behind this process is the governing energy of the vital force.

There are many thousands of similar protective mechanisms continuously at work. We are aware of some of them, but take them totally for granted. Sneezing and coughing help to remove irritants or foreign bodies in the nose, throat or chest. Vomiting and diarrhoea, discharges of mucus and perspiration are all ways of expelling substances from the body which would pose a threat to health. Our bodies keep an even temperature whatever the weather and maintain the right level of sugar, salt, water, and acid/alkali balance in the blood.

It is this homoeostatic balancing act that a herbalist seeks to promote through the use of herbal remedies.

The nature of disease

The vital force is constantly at work to maintain not only the health of the body, but also that of our emotions, and the balance of our mental and spiritual energies.

If outside stresses become too great, the life force may be weakened, and then sickness results. Toxins that are normally expelled start to accumulate in the body. In an attempt to compensate for this, energy is withdrawn from normal day-to-day processes, such as the digestion of food and assimilation of nutrients, and the efforts of the vital force are redirected towards the work of eliminating the waste products through the natural channels — the bowels, kidneys, skin and lungs.

While the body is working so hard in this direction it is wise to assist nature as much as possible. In this instance a herbalist would recommend the patient to desist from eating heavy food to allow energy normally used for digestion to be channelled into the cleansing process. Remedies would not be prescribed to suppress acute vomiting or diarrhoea, or bring down a fever (as long as it had not become life-threatening), as these are natural ways in which the body wards off disease.

Suppression

Suppression of the manifestations of the vital force, such as vomiting and diarrhoea, by inappropriate measures, such as drug treatment, only pushes the illness further into the body. It undermines the work of the vital force and leaves the obstructed organs in a state of chronic disease.

A clear example of this is the excess production of mucus in the nose and throat which results from irritation of the sensitive linings. The mucus acts to dilute the irritants and minimize the damage to the linings, or mucous membranes. If an anti-catarrhal medicine is given this is directly antagonistic to the self-protecting action of the body. The body's strength is thereby depleted and its efforts thwarted, leading to a half-hearted attempt at further elimination and a case of chronic congestion, perhaps leading in turn to chronically infected sinuses.

As the body's energies are worn down by chronic complications, the body is less able to ward off further threats to health, and becomes increasingly predisposed to illness. As the defensive system weakens, the disease can become progressively more serious and eventually life-threatening. A case of childhood eczema which is suppressed will often lead to asthma, as the disease is driven further into the body. Asthma is clearly more life-threatening than a skin condition like excema.

The causes of disease

There are many external influences which can affect the body adversely. As the body's energies are worn down and toxins accumulate, the vital force manifests symptoms in its efforts to combat them.

The herbalist's first job is to look beyond the symptoms to the original cause of the patient's complaint. Causes of illness can be divided into two categories: (i) predisposing causes and (ii) exciting causes. Predisposing causes lower our general health and make us vulnerable to exciting causes, which although usually quite trivial, are 'the last straw which breaks the camel's back'.

To give an example, somebody who lives in the middle of a large city may develop a chronic catarrhal state over a period of time, due to eating too much sugary and starchy food, a lack of fresh air and very little outdoor exercise. Anyone who has an office job could fall into this category. Suddenly the weather gets a lot colder and the person develops a cold, which leads to acute bronchitis. This is blamed on the change of weather but in fact, had it not been for the predisposing causes, the patient would have been able to adapt to the colder weather by homoeostasis without any problem.

Predisposing causes

There are myriad possible predisposing causes for any illness. It may be useful to list here the ones which herbalists consider are most frequently responsible for ill-health:

1. Heredity: We all inherit sensitivities and predispositions from our parents. If your mother has suffered from diabetes, for example, there is a stronger possibility that you will develop it at some stage than if you had no family history of the disease.

2. Nutrition: Eating the wrong kinds of food is a major cause of poor health. The modern diet relies on far too many processed, refined foods — white flour, white sugar, cakes and biscuits, devitalized frozen and canned foods – and over-cooked vegetables. All these foods are lacking in vitamins and minerals, and are unable to provide us with the nutrients we need to keep well and to restore health when we are ill. Many such foods predispose the body to constipation, which will only add to the accumulation of wastes.

3. Stress: Since a person is an integrated whole, stress that affects the mental and emotional state will also undermine physical health, resulting in lowered general vitality. Overwork causes fatigue, as does artificial stimulation from caffeine in tea and coffee, or taking drugs.

Excesses of any kind, burning the candle at both ends, anxiety, tension and trauma can all cause a build-up of stress. Negative states of mind such as anxiety, fear, hatred, envy and mental conflict can upset the central or autonomic nervous system, and it has been shown that these emotions actually lower the defensive action of the

THE POWER OF THE VITAL FORCE

body, predisposing it to infection and inflammatory processes such as arthritis. Eventually they can provoke serious afflictions of the immune system, such as rheumatoid arthritis or even cancer.

4. Toxins: Accumulated wastes and poisons in our bodies cause many problems. Overeating, junk foods, food additives, animal hormones, synthetic stimulants, chemical sprays, smoking and polluted air, the use of drugs, vaccines and sera are among the contributory factors.

5. Occupational factors: Lack of fresh air because of poor ventilation, shallow breathing through sitting hunched up all day, inhalation of toxic fumes and dust at work, exposure to excesses of heat and cold as endured by workers in the building trade, all can impose great stress on our bodies.

6. Radiation: This can accumulate from X-rays, radium treatment, luminous dials, perhaps too much television, and of course nuclear fall-out.

7. Exercise: Many of us spend all day in sedentary occupations, tied to the office desk, and have neither the time nor the inclination to exercise properly. We have become very dependent on our cars and on public transport, and few of us are willing to walk or bicycle more than a short distance.

Lack of exercise means that the circulation becomes inadequate. If we do not work up a sweat every day, one pathway of elimination is not being used productively. Inactive skin function resulting from tight clothing, lack of exercise and infrequent bathing or too frequent hot baths, can all deplete the general health.

Exciting causes
Exciting causes that can trigger illness come in many shapes and forms. The following are a few of the most

familiar factors that push a body already predisposed to illness over the brink:

1. Weather conditions: Sudden changes of weather, extremes of either heat or cold, humidity and strong winds can catch us unawares and trigger incipient illness.

2. Infection: We all catch colds, throat infections, flu and stomach bugs, and perhaps develop 'travellers' diarrhea' when we travel. We blame it on the bacteria or viruses involved, but these only settle and multiply in an environment that provides the right conditions, and where the vitality of life force is not strong enough to fight off the invasions.

3. Trauma: Accidents, injury and mental, emotional or physical shock, even an argument, can upset you enough to lower your defences.

THE PROPERTIES OF HERBS

Medicinal plants are so called because they contain agents that work in the body to prevent or cure illness, in addition to the minerals, vitamins and trace elements present in all plants. The more widely known healing agents are listed below.

Tannins

These substances occur widely in nature and have wonderful healing powers that affect the skin and mucous membranes of the mouth and throughout the digestive, respiratory, urinary and reproductive systems.

The main action of tannins is astringent, and they heal by binding a protein called albumen in the skin and mucosae to form a tight, insoluble protective layer which is resistant to disease. This separates the bacteria which have settled on the skin or mucosae from the source of their nutrition, and also protects against irritation.

Tannins are the predominant healing agent in herbs

such as oak bark, witch hazel, shepherd's purse and herb bennett. They are useful as gargles for sore throats, mouth washes for inflamed gums, medicines for diarrhoea, compresses to heal open wounds and, diluted in hot water, to bathe haemorrhoids and sore and inflamed skin conditions.

Mucilage

This is a substance which is found in many plants, and which swells up when water is added to it, to form a viscous fluid. Marshmallow, flax, comfrey and Iceland moss are all used for their high mucilage content; the mucilage acts to amplify the effect of other healing agents such as tannins, especially in the relief of irritation. It also forms a layer on the surface of the mucous membrane which protects it and rapidly soothes existing irritations and inflammation.

Because of its ability to draw water to it, mucilage can have a slightly laxative effect, as it loosens the bowel content by absorbing water into the bowel. Psyllium seeds work well in cases of constipation. One or two teaspoonsful of the seeds left to soak in a cupful of water for half an hour can be taken night and morning with good effect.

Volatile oils

Most of us are familiar with several plants that contain high concentrations of volatile oils. They are the highly scented herbs grown for culinary purposes — fennel, dill, rosemary, sage, thyme, marjoram and mint. These common herbs impart a pleasant aromatic taste (and smell) to our cooking. But are you aware of what else they can do?

Aromatic essential or volatile oils consist of a wide variety of different compounds, which accounts for the wonderful variation in their smells. Up to 50 components have been identified in a single oil. They also have a wide range of medicinal actions.

All essential oils are natural antiseptics and antibiotics, strengthening our immune systems to ward off bacterial, viral and fungal infection. Many are anti-inflammatory and anti-spasmodic, and are used to relieve cramp, colic and period pains. Several act as expectorants for coughs; as diuretics, increasing the flow of urine; and as tonics to enhance the functions of the stomach, intestines, gallbladder and liver.

When taken in food or drink, or inhaled, volatile oils are distributed rapidly to all parts of the body. Their action is felt throughout the urinary system, the lungs and bronchi, in sweat, saliva, vaginal and lacrimal (from the eye) secretions. In the case of a lactating or pregnant mother, it is carried to the infant or foetus: it can be very helpful for babies with colic if their breast-feeding mother drinks chamomile or fennel tea.

Aromatherapy is the ancient art of healing that uses the aroma of essential oils. When you smell an oil, certain nerve endings situated in the upper part of the nose carry messages to the brain, particularly to the area relating to mental and emotional states. This natural method of treatment is becoming increasingly popular.

Bitters

Some herbs possess healing agents whose potency is related to their bitter qualities. Bitter substances exert their action primarily on the digestive system, stimulating the secretion of digestive juices in the stomach and intestine, and facilitating the flow of bile in the liver. They are excellent for people suffering from loss of appetite and poor digestion. They are used in chronic gastritis, anaemia and nervous exhaustion, and to boost health in convalescence.

Dandelion root, wormwood, gentian, golden seal and centaury are good examples of bitter herbs used to restore strength to someone who has been weakened by ill health. Bitters are often referred to as 'bitter tonics' and, despite many people's dislike of them, for good effect they must be tasted!

Many bitters have other healing properties: some act as sedatives, others stimulate the immune system and are

Angostura bitters, from Angostura

George prefers light and bitter, from the Rose + Crown

MANY OF THE APERITIFS TRADITIONALLY DRUNK BEFORE A MEAL ARE BITTERS, ACTING TO STIMULATE THE FLOW OF DIGESTIVE JUICES AND THEREBY AID DIGESTION..

antibiotic, some are active against tumours, and some have carminative effects, expelling gas from a bloated stomach.

A good illustration is centaury – *Erythraea centaurium* – a wild flower fairly common in temperate climates. Centaury is one of the best bitter wild herbs and acts as a very good general tonic. An infusion of the tops of the plants is often used for a sluggish digestion, heartburn after meals and for lack of appetite. It is a fine tonic for the liver and helps when there is a tendency to obstruction in the liver and gallbladder. Centaury formed the basis of the once famous Portland Powder, which was used to prevent attacks of gout. A decoction of the plant can be used to treat rheumatism, anaemia, and weakness following flu or other more serious and debilitating illness. It is said to strengthen the body generally, and also the mind — it certainly is a helpful addition to prescriptions for nervous disorders.

Alkaloids

These can be very powerful substances and are often toxic when taken in large amounts. For this reason they are usually found only in herbal remedies prepared by qualified medical herbalists according to a legally specified dosage, and are unsuitable for home use in herbal teas.

Alkaloids are organic compounds which contain nitrogen — in other respects they vary widely in components and in action. Atropine, a poison found in deadly nightshade, is an alkaloid, as are morphine (from the opium poppy), caffeine and theobromide in coffees, black tea and cocoa, and nicotine in tobacco. Alkaloids are also found in small amounts in plants not usually regarded as having any poisonous properties, such as comfrey and coltsfoot. Here they serve merely as catalysts for the healing process.

Vitamins, minerals and trace elements

These are vital in the building of connective tissues, bones and teeth, and indeed in the construction of every cell. They form the basis of enzymes and hormones, and are involved in important biochemical processes which control metabolism and the function of every organ in the body.

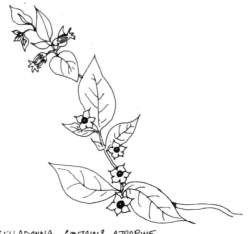

BELLADONNA CONTAINS ATROPINE.

Without vitamins and minerals life could not exist, so it is essential that we receive adequate supplies in our diet. Many popular herbs owe much of their value to their high concentrations of vitamins and minerals. Dandelion, burdock, nettles and dock are all used for their blood-cleansing properties. They are rich in iron, which is vital for good circulation and healthy blood. Nettles also contain silica and potassium, and are used not only for anaemia, but also for skin problems and arthritis.

Healing agents can be found in varying concentrations in different parts of the plant. In spring or summer the most valuable part may be the blossom; at other seasons it may be the leaves, roots, seeds, fruits or even bark. The potency of a herb varies according to the season, the place it is growing and the time of day it is harvested.

WHAT CAN HERBS DO?

All medicinal plants contain a range of different therapeutic agents and therefore have a variety of different actions, related to the combined effect of these components. Sage is a good example: the essential oil in sage leaves, which lends the herb its characteristic odour, is antiseptic and fungicidal. Sage leaves also contain tannin, which is astringent, and a bitter compound called picrosalvine. The disinfectant action of sage tea is due to the combined effect of these components, and is best used in gargles for sore throats, and mouthwashes for inflamed gums.

When the tea is swallowed, other qualities of the plant come into their own. It can act to prevent heavy night-time sweating and stop menopausal flushes and hot sweats. Another use of sage tea is to abate the flow of breast milk when mothers are weaning their babies. The volatile oil in sage contains a substance called thujone. If sage tea is drunk on a regular basis over a long period of time or in large amounts it can bring on menstrual flow, and for this reason it should not be used in pregnancy. However, it can be helpful if a baby is overdue, when it is recommended to stimulate contractions.

Herbs can produce very different effects according to the way they are used. Flax seeds can be ground into a fine powder and used as a compress. They contain a lot of mucilage, which swells and produces a thick paste. When this is hot and applied externally, it acts as a wonderful remedy for chills and pains. When the seeds are soaked in cold water and then taken regularly in the morning or evening, they act as an excellent mechanical laxative. Flax seeds contain an oil which is used in creams to soothe eczema and cradle cap, which can develop on the scalps of small babies. The seeds have a tranquillizing effect when taken internally.

The main actions of herbs

1. They relax tissues or organs which are over-tense, predominantly muscles and the nervous system.
2. They stimulate 'atonic' tissues or organs (those lacking tone), such as a sluggish bowel or liver.
3. They astringe, i.e. they cause constriction of over-relaxed tissues, such as muscles, blood vessels and mucous membranes producing excessive catarrhal secretions.
4. They sedate overactive areas, such as the bowel or nervous system, and lessen functional activity.
5. They promote elimination of wastes and poisons from the liver, bowel, kidneys, lungs and skin.
6. They help overcome infection by stimulating the body's defences and with direct antiseptic, antibiotic and anti-fungal actions.
7. They enhance the circulation of blood and lymph.
8. They aid appetite and digestion and stimulate the absorption and assimilation of nutrients from our diet, as well as providing us with many themselves.
9. They soothe mucous membranes and thereby reduce irritation and inflammation.
10. They regulate the secretion and action of hormones, and where necessary promote hormone production.

3.
WHAT CAN A HERBALIST TREAT?

The word 'heal' comes from the Gothic 'hailjan' and from the Greek word 'holos', both meaning to make whole. Health therefore means wholeness, and it is from this that the term 'holistic healing' is derived. The World Health Organization has defined health as: 'the condition of perfect bodily, spiritual and social well-being, and not solely the absence of illness and injury'.

THE HOLISTIC APPROACH

The type of treatment a practitioner prescribes depends on that practitioner's understanding of the meaning of health. If health is felt to be simply a matter of the subjective well-being of the patient, then almost any means can be employed to eradicate the symptoms — hydrocortisone cream to clear eczema and anti-inflammatory drugs to control arthritis. In seeking to establish the cause of the illness, the practitioner can carry out a purely physiological examination, or go further into the interrelationship between mind, body and spirit. In the case of a practitioner who believes that disease is the manifestation of a disturbed relationship between body and soul, then the imbalance would need to be harmonized through the patient's involvement in a programme of spiritual development, perhaps through a discipline such as yoga or meditation.

The herbalist's approach is to look as closely as possible at the interplay of all aspects of the whole person — physical, emotional, mental and spiritual — and to view the patient's complaint in the context of their findings. The aim is to treat the whole person — but in practice this is not easy, for it is almost impossible to form a complete impression of a patient, let alone to devise a perfect treatment. Still, it does no harm to strive for perfection.

Treating the person — not the disease

Many of the small imbalances that occur between us and our environment are easily sorted out by our homoeostatic mechanisms, as described in the last chapter. When the disruptions to our health are too great, we cannot

TWO PEOPLE WITH ARTHRITIS MAY MANIFEST SIMILAR SYMPTOMS BUT THEY ARE NOT THE SAME PEOPLE.

rebalance ourselves and a state of ill-health develops, progressing to either acute or chronic disease.

Just as each one of us is different, so we all react differently to imbalance and disharmony. It is important to look at each case individually and treat the person, not the disease. Two people with arthritis may appear to manifest similar symptoms, but they are not the same: their lives, their personalities, their emotional and spiritual make-up, and thus the causes of their illness, will probably be completely different. These factors will determine the treatment given — no two prescriptions by a herbalist are likely to be exactly the same.

The herbalist's first concern is to find out as much as possible about the patient's temperament, constitution and lifestyle, in order to discover areas of weakness that may be subject to stress and strain, causing disease. What a medical herbalist is looking for is not so much a label for a disease, such as high blood pressure, duodenal ulcer or arthritis, as the underlying causes of the patient's ill-health.

WHAT HELP CAN A HERBALIST OFFER?

Having established that a herbalist aims to treat the cause, not the symptoms, the patient and not the disease, it would be true to say that a herbalist can treat anybody. The purpose of herbal medication is to act as a catalyst for the patient's own healing energies, aiding recovery from a particular complaint while giving a boost to the convalescent's general health.

Some progressive diseases are declared incurable. Even though a herbalist may not be able to cure somebody suffering from Parkinson's disease or multiple sclerosis, the herbs will certainly raise the patient's level of vitality and improve emotional, mental and perhaps spiritual life.

To aim to cure the physical symptoms is perhaps to take a shortsighted view of the deeper meaning of illness. Symptoms are nature's way of telling us something is wrong in our lives. Perhaps we should be grateful to them for their ability to teach us something about ourselves, whi:h we then can change for the better. If we are too eager to suppress our symptoms we may never have the opportunity of learning some of the more difficult and valuable lessons of life.

Life demands that we constantly change and evolve. Disease occurs when our evolution or growth is somehow blocked or hampered. Disease is a sign that something in our life needs to be changed; its suppression stops harmonious evolution.

The conventional approach to pain illustrates this quite clearly. We are brought up to feel that pain is a negative thing and we are given pain-killing drugs to eliminate it. We are thereby denying our inner being the chance to warn us that we are misusing ourselves to some degree. If pain has developed to the point of being unbearable, drugs can certainly be useful, but if its cause had been ascertained at the onset the chances are that it would never have reached this intensity. True relief of pain is only gained by removal of its cause.

Suppression of pain may also deprive us of the chance to develop as human beings. The human relationship to pain and suffering is important in all the great religions of the world, and some even regard it as a gift for the wisdom it can bring us. The automatic suppression of pain deprives us of the chance to experience this.

CHRONIC AND ACUTE PROBLEMS

In practice the type of illness that a herbalist encounters from day to day tends to be chronic rather than acute. Most people suffering from acute problems such as throat or chest infections are generally satisfied with the fact that antibiotics appear to have the desired effect and work very well. They do not realize that suppressing the acute problem may predispose them to a more chronic one. Only once illness has become chronic do most people begin to be aware of the drawbacks of ignoring its underlying causes, and of the damage caused by suppression.

People with chronic illness are on the whole considerably less satisfied with conventional treatment, either because it does not relieve the problem or because of unpleasant side-effects. It is at this point that they often begin their search for alternatives such as herbal medicine.

An increasing number of people are in sympathy with a natural approach to healing. They and their families choose to consult a herbalist with their acute problems instead of going through orthodox channels first. One drawback with the treatment of acute disease by herbalism is that it is a private system of medicine where practitioners tend to work singly rather than in groups, and are thus unable to be on call at all times of the day and night as doctors are. Inevitably, acute problems can arise outside consulting hours, and may then have to be dealt with by a general practitioner.

Typical acute problems

- Colds, sore throats, ear and eye infections, fevers, coughs, croup, bronchitis, rhinitis and sinusitis.
- All kinds of allergic reactions, skin rashes, hay fever, eczema and asthma.
- Gastric disorders and infections, bowel problems.
- Cystitis and kidney infections.
- Arthritis.
- Headaches.
- Chillblains.
- Glandular fever and other infections.

Typical chronic problems

- Headaches and migraine.
- Heart and circulatory disorders such as angina, arteriosclerosis, chillblains, varicose veins and high blood pressure.
- Cystitis and kidney disorders.
- Digestive problems such as gastritis, piles, hiatus hernia, peptic ulcers, constipation, diverticulitis, gallstones, colitis and irritable bowel syndrome.

- Respiratory problems such as bronchitis, pleurisy, asthma, rhinitis and sinusitis.
- Rheumatism, arthritis and gout.
- Skin problems such as acne, eczema and psoriasis.
- A wide variety of nervous problems — stress and anxiety, insomnia, debility, panic attacks, depression, agoraphobia, claustrophobia, multiple sclerosis, Parkinson's disease and shingles.
- Hormonal problems, menopausal problems, prostate problems, premenstrual tension and menstrual difficulties such as dysmenorrhea.
- Gynaecological problems such as endometriosis, infections and inflammatory conditions, infertility, problems during pregnancy and post-natal depression.
- Children's problems: chronic upper respiratory infections, tonsillitis, hyperactivity, allergies, bed wetting and colic.
- Infections such as thrush, athlete's foot, boils, herpes and mastitis.

Patients with serious, life-threatening illnesses such as cancer, cataracts, diabetes, epilepsy, glaucoma, glomerulonephritis, paralysis, tuberculosis, and sexually transmitted diseases may choose to be treated conventionally. At the same time there is nothing to stop them from taking herbal medicines to improve their general health and vitality.

THE DIAGNOSIS

Many people are concerned about whether or not a medical herbalist is able adequately to diagnose disease, and wonder if it would be advisable first to consult their doctor for an accurate diagnosis.

Qualified herbalists have been trained in all the basic medical sciences — physiology, anatomy, pathology and differential diagnosis — and have passed a theoretical as well as a clinical exam in physical examination techniques and diagnosis. They should have the basic tools of medical diagnosis — a stethoscope, a sphygmomanometer for taking blood pressure, an opthalmoscope for examining the eyes, an otoscope for the ears, a haemoglobinometer to check for anaemia. In addition, some carry out urine analysis.

If you visit your doctor first, as prospective patients frequently do, you may well be given a disease label — such as depression or rheumatism — which can cover a very wide range of symptoms. I have encountered several people who have been prescribed anti-depressants when actually what they have is a hormonal imbalance or an allergy. This is why it can be misleading to visit a doctor before consulting a herbalist, because the two practitioners have radically different approaches.

Having said this, if your herbalist considers that further investigation is necessary, you may be advised to return to your doctor for referral to a specialist who can carry out more sophisticated tests, such as X-rays, liver function tests, or electrocardiograms.

SELF-HELP

Herbal medicine is the form of alternative medicine most widely used in the home. Not so long ago most country people had favourite herbal remedies which they used to treat minor acute problems, thereby preventing them from developing into more serious or chronic disease. Most families had only a limited knowledge of home-doctoring, but this was backed up by the strong relationship between home and the family doctor. Herbs were part of family life.

As medicine has increased in technological complexity, most simple plant medicines have gradually fallen out of use in the home. Faith in the progress of medical science has meant that formerly self-sufficient people have grown to believe that only sophisticated drugs are appropriate and adequate for proper medical care. Most families have

relinquished their skills in home-medication and first aid, and consult their doctor for the simplest of minor health problems.

This means that we are cut adrift from our roots, and have lost the self-esteem associated with reliance on our own skills. People no longer feel that they have control over the fate of their own bodies. We have handed responsibility for our health to the medical profession. This passivity is proving to be a great mistake, yet the bad habits that we have developed are hard to break.

Among the first to want to break the habits of the recent past have been older people who still remember herbalism as a simple, harmless form of medicine that was practised in their families. These people may have been given a 'disease label', such as arthritis or peptic ulcer by their doctors, or they may have made their own diagnosis of a simple problem. In either case they are looking for something natural to replace the prospect of drugs. They have turned to the health food shops, which now stock an increasingly wide range of herbal remedies.

However great your enthusiasm for instant remedies to treat any problem, it is important to bear in mind that the first signs of serious illness can be deceptively mild. For simple minor ailments that do not persist or recur, and for first aid, herbal medicine bought over the counter may well help. But for those symptoms which do not disappear, or for any problem which has already been diagnosed as a more serious illness, a trained herbal practitioner should be consulted.

Herbal remedies bought over the counter can be used in a symptomatic way, i.e. to treat the arthritis or the ulcer without seeking the underlying causes for the problem. The justification for using herbal remedies in this way is that they are natural rather than synthetic products, and therefore free of side-effects (see p. 19). However, it is rather a hit or miss approach, and does no justice at all to the art of the trained herbalist who will treat the cause, not just the symptoms, and the person, not just the disease. It may also lead to disappointment in the healing power of herbs.

Rather than using proprietary herbal medicines to treat an already established problem, it is much better to use herbs at home as preventive medicine. If herbs are used in food and cooking they can be incorporated into our daily lives without being taken as medicines. Choose them according to your needs and their medical properties. If you are aware of a tendency to develop frequent colds in winter, which settle on the chest, then you can use herbs that have an affinity to chest problems and others that benefit the immune system.

Garlic, especially raw garlic, is very beneficial to the immune system and the bronchial system, and can be added to salads or even sandwiches, as long as you don't mind the pungent aroma. Lemon juice can be added to salad dressings; honey, cloves or angelica to puddings; and comfrey and plantain leaves can be chopped and added to salads or cooked as spinach. Thyme is delicious in stews or salads, and borage and mallow flowers can be used as edible decoration on salad, casseroles and puddings.

HOW SAFE IS NATURAL?

Natural herbal remedies are clearly less harmful than chemical drugs. However, it is a mistake to suppose that natural means completely safe in any amount. There are some herbs which must be treated with great respect and care.

There are now many books available on herbal medicine extolling the virtues of herbs. The illustrations and descriptions of the plants may easily encourage people to start looking around in their gardens and the surrounding countryside for herbs to gather and prepare for medicinal use. This can be a tricky business, as you must be absolutely sure of the identity of the plant before using it.

The ideal way to treat yourself at home for minor problems is with the support of a qualified herbalist, to whom you can refer when in doubt on any account.

When not to treat yourself

It is advisable to consult a herbalist in the following circumstances:

- If an illness or symptoms have persisted for more than a few days.
- If the patient has suffered from continual or acute pain.
- If sudden changes for the worse occur in the patient's condition.
- If home treatment has actually produced good results, but the patient relapses once the treatment is stopped.
- If there is no improvement at all in the patient's condition after the first few days of treatment.

Symptoms of many serious illnesses do not appear serious in themselves, especially in the early stages. It is often impossible for an unqualified person correctly to interpret the symptoms, especially if the patient has been receiving drug treatment. When in doubt, do not attempt home treatment.

4.
A VISIT TO THE HERBALIST

WHY DO PEOPLE COME?

People consult herbalists for a variety of reasons. The majority of patients have a chronic disorder, which has been treated unsuccessfully elsewhere, and are looking for an alternative. They have heard or read that herbal medicine may offer a cure, safely, gently and without side-effects.

Many people do not make the decision to try herbalism until all else has failed and they are desperate. Their condition is often fairly advanced, and is complicated by the effects of the medicines they have been prescribed. Naturally these patients can be difficult to treat and recovery is slow. Many are looking for a miracle cure. Even if they have been ill for 15-20 years and taking drugs without significant improvement, once they embark on herbal treatment they often expect results within a few weeks or even days.

Some patients have been taking drugs such as tranquillizers, anti-depressants and anti-hypertensives (for high blood pressure) for many years, and face the prospect of continuing to take them for the rest of their lives. Naturally, they would like to consider the possibility of coming off them.

Others are taking or have taken medicines and suffered unpleasant side-effects. They are wary of a recurrence of their problem and are seeking a more gentle alternative that is without risks. Many patients, especially those with symptoms which do not fit a classic disease picture and those with nervous, hormonal or allergic complaints, feel misunderstood and they really need time to talk. Their doctor is probably very overworked and lacks the time to listen. Listening is an important part of the herbalist's job.

A large number of people have relatively minor problems for which they are being treated with what they consider unnecessarily powerful medicines. They believe, for example, that herbal medicine offers a more suitable treatment for childhood eczema and inflamed eyes than cortisone. Parents are worried by recurring childhood problems such as sore throats, ear and chest infections, for which antibiotics are regularly prescribed. They would prefer their children to be given gentler medication, and above all they want to establish the root of the problem so that a more lasting cure can be found.

As people are becoming more aware of themselves, increasingly wanting to take responsibility for their own health, so they are tending more and more to consult herbalists as a first line of treatment. They may feel merely under the weather, tired and a little run-down, with vague symptoms, which they would like to resolve before they develop further. Many would like to analyse their state of health in relation to their diet, environment and lifestyle, and simply need a sounding-board. Others are just curious. They may have heard a friend or relative sing the praises of their local herbalist, and are interested in seeing for themselves.

HOW TO FIND A HERBALIST

There are growing numbers of people who feel disillusioned with modern medicine, but who know little about the world of holistic medicine. Though my husband and I have been in our present practice for six years now, we frequently encounter people living locally who have only recently heard about our work and exclaim: 'If only I had known about you before, I would have come years ago!' Even those who have long been interested in treating themselves with herbs may have no idea of the existence of medical herbalism as a profession.

THERE ARE GROWING NUMBERS OF PEOPLE WHO FEEL DISILLUSIONED WITH MODERN MEDICINE.

This lack of information is disappearing fast. Holistic or alternative medicine has recently enjoyed wide coverage on radio and television, and in newspapers and magazines. In fact health magazines abound, and every woman's magazine has regular articles on health and fitness the natural way.

However, many still regard natural medicine with some degree of scepticism and mistrust, especially if they are seriously ill. People may wish to try something other than conventional medicine, but unless they actually know somebody who has attended a holistic practice, they feel wary about making the first step. It is almost as if it were a club to which they do not belong.

So the majority of people who consult a herbalist have heard about herbal medicine through word of mouth. We treat many people who have travelled a long way to see us, preferring to see somebody who has been personally recommended to them rather than a completely unknown practitioner who may live nearby.

It is clearly comforting to have seen somebody else's health improve through herbal treatment before trying it yourself. Some patients have even said to me, 'I'll see how

61

I get on with your treatment, and if I get better I'll send my husband and daughter along to you.' And this is exactly what happens.

For those who have neither eager friends nor exuberant neighbours to introduce herbalism to them and recommend a practitioner, you can ask at your local health food shop whether there is a herbalist nearby. Herbalists may be listed in the telephone directory. Your local doctor may also be able to inform you about practitioners in the area, and may even refer you personally.

Qualifications to look for
Herbalists have worked for hundreds of years without having to qualify at a particular standard of knowledge and expertise. This means that in theory anybody can set up as a herbal practitioner. There are *bona fide* amateur herbalists whose aim is to spread the word about the healing powers of herbs, and treat simple ailments of friends and relatives. But a word of warning – beware of quacks!

If you need to consult a qualified herbalist whose training is adequate to ensure correct diagnosis and competent treatment of your problem, then make sure they belong to a recognized official body, such as the National Institute of Medical Herbalists (with the letters MNIMH or FNIMH after their name).

BOOKING AN APPOINTMENT

Unlike doctors, most practising herbalists do not have clinics, where patients attend between certain hours and wait their turn to be seen. Consultations are usually long, and so herbalists operate by appointment only.

At our practice, people who do not realize the importance of the consultation often ask whether they can just collect a herbal remedy for some specific illness. If they are new to herbalism, they may not be aware that herbalists and doctors approach their patients in very different ways. We have to explain that, by law, we are unable to make up a prescription for a patient we have not seen; and, secondly, that our aim is to treat the patient as a whole, which means putting health problems – even small ones like sore toes – into the context of lifestyles, so that we can treat causes and not just symptoms. This requires a fairly lengthy initial consultation. Naturally, when people approach a herbalist through recommendation by others, they are more aware of what to expect.

All appointments are booked in advance. People either visit the practice to fix a time, or more often telephone and speak to a receptionist or directly to the practitioner. Depending on how busy the herbalist is, you may have to book four to six weeks in advance.

Some people feel that once they have made the decision to 'phone and make an appointment, they ought to 'strike while the iron is hot' and be seen tomorrow. This is not usually possible unless there has been a last-minute cancellation. So 'book early to avoid disappointment'!

WHAT DOES IT COST?

It varies widely and depends a great deal on the herbalist's training. In this country there is no standardization of training for professional herbalists. This leads to wide discrepancies in the educational background of practitioners. A fully qualified physician may include herbal treatments in a medical practice. On the other hand, someone who is simply interested in the subject and knowledgeable about this form of healing may set up in practice. Both of these practitioners will, of course, have very different fees. Therefore, when asking about the cost of therapy, you might also wish to establish the herbalist's credentials.

Most herbalists operate a sliding scale of charges, and for students, the unemployed, elderly retirees and anybody having a tough time financially, fees can normally be reduced to suit both the patient and the practitioner. Never let the finances put you off consulting a herbalist. Most herbalists are more concerned with their patients' health than with money, as long as they can make ends meet.

In addition to the consultation fee there is the cost of the herbal medicine, which could range from $6 - $20 per week for the basic herbal mixture, and sometimes more if there are extra lotions, ointments or tablets.

The cost of the medicine reflects the fact that many medicinal herbs are in short supply as wild areas of countryside are being taken over by farms, houses, roads and motorways, as well as being destroyed by pollution. Harvests can fail, and many herbs are actually becoming extinct. Destruction of the tropical forests in South America is also a serious problem, as countless species are being wiped out before even being discovered, let alone investigated.

Herbs take time to be harvested and labour is not cheap. However, the cost of herbal remedies is still comparatively small.

PREPARING FOR THE FIRST VISIT

Given that the initial consultation is going to be fairly lengthy, especially when compared to a visit to a doctor or specialist, you can safely assume that the herbalist will want to ask you a number of questions.

It is worth thinking about, or even making a note of, your past medical history, illnesses and operations, going right back to childhood or infancy. You may need to consult your family to jog your memory. It is even worth discovering if you were breastfed and for how long. The state of your general health in childhood and the treatment you received for various illnesses can have a considerable bearing upon your adult health. It is useful to have all the facts at the ready to avoid wasting time or missing out important pieces of information.

It can be useful to the practitioner if you keep a diary of all that you eat and drink through the day for a couple of days prior to the visit. The herbalist can then analyse your diet at a glance without having to go through it bit by bit at the interview.

Some people have difficulty answering questions. If you get confused easily or suffer from loss of memory or a nervous disorder, then you should take a friend or relative along with you, to whom the herbalist can refer if necessary.

If you are able to bring along any medical reports that you have from doctors, specialists, or holistic therapists, such as X-rays, blood and urine analyses or allergy tests, then naturally this is helpful.

You should be aware that a herbalist will not only inquire into your previous medical history, but also needs to have some idea of your mental and emotional state, past and present. Some people may have to prepare themselves inwardly for this, as it may be hard to talk about something that is still painful to dwell on, perhaps a death in the family, the break-up of a relationship or difficulties within a marriage.

Otherwise there is little else that needs to be done in the way of preparation before seeing a herbalist — just come with an open mind! Avoid wearing corsets and girdles for the consultation, as they take a long time to take off and put back on, and as with a doctor a physical examination will sometimes be necessary. If you are on prescribed medicine, continue to take it as usual before your visit.

THE INITIAL CONSULTATION

As a patient, you will be greeted by the receptionist or dispenser and shown into the waiting room. It may be a busy joint practice or the quiet clinic of a single practitioner, but the atmosphere will be friendly and reassuring. There will usually be flowers, noticeboards to

THE WAITING ROOM

read and magazines to browse through. In some ways it will be similar to any other waiting room, except that the information and magazines will have a decidedly natural slant and the patients may be talking to one another rather than sitting together in tense silence.

In our waiting room at our home practice — a cottage in the middle of beautiful Cotswold countryside — we have large windows overlooking the colourful garden where we grow many of the herbs which make up our patients' medicines. In summer, patients are invited to look around the garden or relax there while they wait for their appointment, or afterwards while their medicines are being prepared.

There are a couple of noticeboards with newspaper cuttings relevant to herbalism and other natural therapies. There are piles of health magazines to read, decorative charts, pictures and certificates on the wall, and a bookshelf full of books on herbal medicine and allied subjects, which patients may dip into if they wish.

People come in and go out, bringing herbs they have gathered, collecting repeat prescriptions or making appointments. The waiting room always seems a busy place.

IN THE PRACTICE ROOM

On entering a herbalist's practice room some people may be comforted to find it not dissimilar to a doctor's office, though there are subtle differences. It is perhaps not as clinical, but there is always a desk at which the practitioner sits, and the evidence of medical training such as stethoscope, sphygmomanometer, ophthalmoscope, otoscope and haemoglobinometer. You may see reference books. There is also usually an examination couch and often a wash-basin.

Every herbalist endeavours to produce a warm, relaxing and inviting atmosphere. The room will very much reflect the individual practitioner's approach to healing. There are often vases of herbs and flowers, perhaps pictures of plants on the walls, bookshelves of medical and herbal tomes, and shelves with other necessary equipment such as examination gloves, specula, oils for massage and kidney bowls.

THE HERBALIST'S PRACTICE ROOM

THE INTERVIEW

As the herbalist greets you and takes down details of your name, address, age and occupation, an assessment is already beginning to form. Your general appearance can divulge plenty about you. Are you untidy, or fastidious, with not a hair out of place? Do you wear a lot of make-up or are you very natural? Are you poor or wealthy, fashion-conscious or individualistic?

Then there is body language — the drawn face and slumped shoulders of someone unhappy or downtrodden; the clenched hands, raised shoulders and perhaps slightly pursed mouth of someone who is tense, and 'stiff upper-lip'; the anxious and imploring eyes of someone desperate for help; the distorted gait of somebody obviously suffering from Parkinson's disease.

The complexion and eyes, the colour of the lips, the shine of the hair and the state of the fingernails can all tell their own story. Don't be alarmed, but your consultation has begun the minute you walk into the room.

Some herbalists use printed case-history sheets, which they fill in as your story unfolds; others simply use a notepad. The actual interview begins as the herbalist asks the purpose of your visit — what your main problem is, and what help you would like. This gives you the opportunity to describe your condition in whatever detail you like. The practitioner will ask about your symptoms be they physical, emotional or mental. You will probably feel more comfortable describing your physical symptoms first, as you will be weighing up the herbalist (as well as being weighed up yourself) to find out whether he or she has a sympathetic ear, is a good listener, seems to care, is competent and to be trusted, and understands the problem.

So the two of you will discuss your physical symptoms, when they first started, in relation to which events (perhaps after moving house, a shock, a change of some kind, an injury), at which times the symptoms are better or worse, and factors that aggravate or relieve them.

The herbalist may then seek to establish the existence of other associated conditions. For example, a female patient may come with acne, an ugly and disfiguring skin complaint which affects the back, the chest and especially the face. She says her skin is better in the sun and worse under stress and tension, and when she is overworking. She has noticed that it also flares up just before her period, and clears slightly afterwards. The condition began when she started menstruating at the age of 11, and she is now 22. The acne is showing no sign of disappearing. When the herbalists questions her, she says the only other symptoms she has are cold fingers and toes, especially in winter, and period problems. She suffers from bad premenstrual tension for one week before her period with swollen and tender breasts, and a bloated abdomen and pain on the first day.

What she does not realize is that this particular skin complaint is closely related to hormone balance. Her period problems indicate clearly that she has a hormonal imbalance, and it is significant that the acne began around the time of her first period. But why are her hormones imbalanced? This is what the herbalist will try to discover in the interview.

Previous medical history

The herbalist will inquire into the patient's past medical history and treatments prescribed. Here the patient can refer to notes made previously if necessary. This information makes an important contribution to the almost detective-like work the herbalist has to carry out in ascertaining the underlying causes of the patient's illness. It gives a clear picture of the chain of events leading to the patient's present state of health, where apparently unrelated conditions can actually be surprisingly relevant — such as the fact that the patient has had a lifelong history of constipation, has had to take laxatives for years and has now developed rheumatoid arthritis.

The kind of treatment the patient has previously been prescribed is also important. It gives an idea of how far the efforts of the vital force have been suppressed, and how one illness has developed into another (constipation into arthritis, eczema into asthma). It indicates how long the patient may take to recover. It also helps to differentiate between the symptoms associated with the initial complaint, and those brought about by the drugs prescribed to treat it (so-called iatrogenic disease), which can be very hard to distinguish.

Family history
The herbalist may move on to consider the health of other members of the family to obtain an indication of how far the patient's condition is related to inherited predispositions. Information about the family's health also gives a pointer towards the general vitality of the patient, and helps to determine the prognosis.

Other general questions
Returning to the present to paint a fuller picture of the patient's health, the herbalist may enquire about the vital functions of the body beginning with the digestive system, and ask about appetite, any problems with digestion and the nature of bowel movements. The respiratory system might be next on the agenda, with questions about breathing difficulties, coughs and congestion, followed by the circulatory, urinary and reproductive systems. There may often be questions about sleep patterns, perhaps even about dreams.

It is essential that the herbalist assesses each of the body's systems to determine whether the condition has as its origin either over- or under-function, so that treatment can be prescribed that will aid rather than oppose the natural healing function of the body.

THE PHYSICAL EXAMINATION
The herbalist may now need to perform a physical

examination. A routine procedure could include taking the pulse and blood pressure, checking the heart and lungs, observing the tongue and looking into the eyes. Depending on the type of condition that is presented by the patient, the herbalist may then examine more specific areas – such as the ears, the throat, the abdomen, the nervous system reflexes, skin lesions or varicose veins. Many herbalists also carry out gynaecological examinations.

Once the examination is over, a clearer picture of the physical health of the patient will have emerged. The herbalist may ask for a urine sample, or take a blood sample for analysis. The patient could be referred to his or her doctor for further tests requiring sophisticated equipment, such as X-rays or electrocardiograms, to augment the herbalist's diagnosis, especially if something serious such as cancer, heart or kidney disease is suspected.

The physical examination can also serve another purpose. It allows for physical contact between practitioner and patient, which can act as a great ice-breaker. Many people feel inhibited about exposing their bodies to a stranger, even though that stranger might be a doctor, and they like even less the idea of being touched by one. However, touch is a wonderful way of transmitting warmth, sympathy and care for the patient, as well as reassurance. This helps to pave the way for the next part of the consultation.

ESTABLISHING THE UNDERLYING CAUSES
In most uncomplicated case histories, the interview now moves on to a more informal talk about the patient's life. The herbalist will enquire about the environment in which the patient lives and works, daily habits of work and relaxation, exercise, interest and hobbies, friends and family, marital and sexual relationships. The patient now has an opportunity to discuss the stresses encountered in

daily life, personal happiness and satisfaction, anxieties and tensions, and traumas past and present.

The picture that is built up from this interchange shows the herbalist the person behind the disease, revealing the deeper levels from which the illness probably springs to be exhibited in physical symptoms. The form this part of the consultation takes depends very much on the approach of the practitioner and the developing relationship between practitioner and patient. Some people are more ready to talk about themselves than others, and may begin to do so almost straightaway. A more reluctant patient, or one with extensive and complicated physical problems, may be asked back for a second interview to discuss personal matters.

Most people are happy to open up. Very often treatment starts as soon as the patient begins to talk, shedding anxiety and unhappiness that may have been bottled up inside without a suitable outlet, creating an inner imbalance and triggering the physical symptoms.

The herbalist is eminently suited to the role of listener, being neither family nor friend and having the ability to remain objective. Everything is told in strictest confidence, so there are no repercussions.

It may be that what is revealed at this stage of the consultation requires other kinds of therapy to supplement herbal treatment. A herbalist will often recommend relaxation techniques, perhaps breathing exercises, or yoga, t'ai chi, meditation or self-awareness techniques. Alternatively, the patient may be advised to consult a psychotherapist or family therapist, hypnotist or other holistic practitioner, if the treatment required is beyond the realms of the herbalist.

A WORD ABOUT FOOD

Nutrition plays a major part in health and disease, so it is essential for the herbalist to assess the patient's eating habits. This is easily accomplished by questions or by analysis of a food diary which the patient may have brought along. 'You are what you eat' is a notion that can be totally bewildering to newcomers to natural medicine.

Very often a dramatic change in eating habits is called for. Many people find changing their diet difficult. Some even feel that the ground is being taken from under their feet if it is suggested that the Sunday roast and daily meat and two vegetables is not the best thing for, say, arthritis, or that eight to ten cups of coffee a day do nothing to help anxiety and tension.

There are general rules about nutrition that the herbalist will explain to each patient whose diet falls short. A wholesome diet with plenty of fresh fruit and vegetables, seeds, nuts, beans and legumes is recommended for all. A diet sheet will frequently be given out to this effect. Additionally, there are specific suggestions as to what to eat and what to avoid for particular conditions. For example, rhubarb, spinach, tomatoes and oranges are wholesome nutritious foods, full of vitamins, minerals and trace elements, but they are not recommended for people with arthritis, kidney stones or cystitis.

THE SUNDAY ROAST MAY NOT BE THE BEST THING FOR YOUR HEALTH.

73

It may be that an allergic reaction to certain foods is sparking off a particular condition, such as migraine, asthma, rheumatoid arthritis, eczema or persistent congestion problems. It is important to ascertain what foods are implicated before attempting to treat the underlying condition causing the allergy. The herbalist will advise on techniques to analyse allergies, and explain the way to go about changing one's eating habits accordingly.

AT THE END OF THE CONSULTATION

By the end of the allotted time the herbalist should have developed a fairly detailed and colourful picture of the patient's life and physical, emotional and mental condition. Perhaps the picture might be sketchy in places, but the gaps will be filled in on subsequent visits. Obviously the more the patient is able to tell the herbalist, the easier it should be to prescribe treatment. Often a vital piece of the jigsaw will slip out just as the patient is leaving, such as: 'By the way, perhaps I should have told

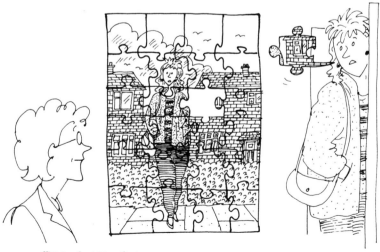

... OFTEN A VITAL PIECE OF THE JIGSAW WILL BE LET SLIP JUST AS THE PATIENT IS LEAVING ...

you, I'm fighting a lawsuit at the moment,' or simply: 'I'm taking an important examination in three weeks' time.'

The herbalist now has a sufficiently clear idea of what treatment is needed, and proceeds to make up the prescription. The patient is asked to return shortly, usually in a week or two, depending on the condition. If the problem is acute, the patient may be asked to report back in a couple of days.

5.
THE
TREATMENT

Herbalists can either buy their remedies from the numerous manufacturers and suppliers of botanical medicines, or they can make them up themselves. Most do both.

HERBS — THE RAW INGREDIENTS

Many of the herbs that are used in daily practice are simple wild flowers that grow in abundance in the countryside, or even in our gardens.

As herbalists who live in the country, one of the joys of our work is to go out collecting our remedies. In our garden we are able to grow several of the herbs we use, and many of our patients are only too happy to gather 'weeds' from their own land to bring to us. Perhaps it connects them more closely to the particular form of therapy they have chosen. The lanes and hedgerows abound with medicinal herbs, and there is something very therapeutic about going out in the morning once the dew has dried off the plants, and gathering them for the purpose of healing.

The hours spent collecting the herbs lend an extra dimension of insight into herbal medicine. By observing the way the plant grows and its habitat, it is possible to broaden one's knowledge of the essence of herbs and their healing powers, and to see the plant in a way that science never does, with intuitive perception.

Other remedies have to be imported from abroad,

THE LANES AND HEDGEROWS AROUND US ABOUND WITH MEDICINAL HERBS...

perhaps from India or South America. In this case it is necessary to buy in the herbs from a supplier.

MAKING UP THE REMEDIES

Herbal remedies can be given in many different forms. The most prevalent is the dried form, which can be used to make tinctures, teas and tablets.

Herbal tinctures

These are fairly concentrated extracts of herbs, and their preparation involves the use of a mixture of water and alcohol, which draws out the chemical constituents of the plants. The alcohol also acts as a preservative.

When making up a tincture, the herbalist refers to herbal pharmacopeia where the ratio of water and alcohol used in the mixture is specified. This differs from one herb to another, depending on the constituents of the plant that need to be extracted. It can be anything from 25 per cent alcohol for simple glycosides and tannins, to 90 per cent alcohol for resins and gums. The required herb, either fresh or dried, is chopped or powdered, then

THE TREATMENT

placed in a large jar, and the water and alcohol solution is poured over it. If a dried herb is used, normally one part of plant is used to every five parts of water. If fresh plants are used the ratio is one to two.

An airtight lid is placed on the jar and the contents are left to macerate away from direct sunlight for no less than two weeks, and shaken daily. After this time the mixture is ready to be pressed. The healing agents should have been absorbed into the solution and the herb itself is no longer necessary.

Most of the liquid can be poured straight off into a bottle, then the rest containing the herb is put into a muslin bag and placed in a press. Pressure is applied gently and the liquid is gradually squeezed out of the plant until it is practically dry. The plant can then be discarded. Some amount of the fluid is lost in each pressing, as it is not possible to squeeze out every last drop from the plant. The tincture is then transferred to dark storage bottles and put in a cool place to be used for topping up the dispensary bottles.

A few tinctures can be prepared using cider vinegar. The acetic acid acts as a solvent that is particularly suited to some herbs, such as lobelia and squill bulb. Some people may be familiar with herbal vinegars used in the kitchen, such as rosemary and tarragon, or with raspberry vinegar, which is commonly used for coughs and sore throats.

To avoid the alcohol content in tinctures, some herbalists prefer to prescribe glycerol-based preparations. Glycerol lends a syrupy taste to the medicine, making it excellent for children and sweet-toothed adults – peppermint and elderflower are excellent used in this way. This method is also useful for herbs with a high mucilage content, but glycerol is not as good an extractor as alcohol for resins, gums and oils. Equal parts of glycerol (of plant origin) and water are poured over the herb, and otherwise the process is the same as for alcoholic tinctures.

Administration of herbs in tincture form has several advantages. The medicines are easy to store and to dispense. They keep extremely well and they are not at

79

risk in damp or cold. Because they are fairly concentrated, the patient only has to take very small amounts of the medicine at intervals through the day.

Infusions and decoctions

Infusions and decoctions are an alternative to tinctures. They can be made by the patient from herbs dispensed by the herbalist. They are drunk by the cupful since they are less concentrated than tinctures.

This method of administration involves more time and effort on the part of the patient and may also involve some unpleasantness, because many herbal remedies are extremely bitter and some could even be said to taste foul. It is of course a matter of taste. The British and the Americans tend to prefer sweet things, whereas African and Jamaican patients actually enjoy bitter remedies.

Most herbals for the lay person advocate the use of infusions and decoctions in preference to other methods. In Europe there is a strong tradition of drinking infusions or 'tisanes', as the French call them. Until recently, this habit was less popular in Britain. In France, Italy, Spain and Greece, tisanes of peppermint, chamomile, elderflower, lemon balm and limeflower are drunk as a matter of course. In Italy bitter aperitifs are taken before eating to stimulate the flow of digestive juices.

Infusions and decoctions are popular among patients who enjoy participating directly in their own therapy, though some people do look slightly dismayed when they are given leaves or flowers to make into a tea, or roots to boil.

Modern orthodox medicine is partly to blame as it has encouraged the patient to believe that the only thing necessary for recovery is to pop a pill at the specified time. Obviously the herbalist has to choose the right patient to whom to prescribe infusions and decoctions.

Infusions are used for the soft parts of plants — leaves, stems, and flowers, while decoctions are used for roots and herbs containing hard, woody material.

Preparing an infusion

Infusions are prepared like normal teas. Either fresh or dried herbs can be used, singly or in mixtures, though fresh herbs need to be used in greater quantities because of their water content. One teaspoon of the dried herb can be used per cup of boiling water. The herbs are placed in an ordinary teapot and boiling water is poured over them and left to infuse for 10-15 minutes.

Teas are usually drunk hot, especially when treating fevers, colds, and congestion, and lukewarm to cold for any problems associated with the urinary tract — cystitis, kidney infections, stones and gravel. The drink can be sweetened with honey if you wish.

Herbal tea bags are sold in almost all health food shops and are a good, healthy substitute for ordinary tea and coffee. They are usually made from the more pleasant-tasting aromatic herbs such as mint, lemon balm, fennel, vervain and limeflowers, and various exotic combinations

81

are available. Of course, you can create your own mixtures to taste.

If larger quantities of herbs need to be made up, the normal dosage is 25g/1oz dried herb to 600ml/1 pint boiling water. However, this is often impractical as most herbal teas are best taken hot and they do not keep for very long, even in the fridge.

If the herbs are aromatic with a high volatile oil content, the tea should be infused in a teapot with a tightly fitting lid to ensure that the oil does not escape with the steam.

Some herbs need to be made up as a cold infusion, since their valuable chemical constituents are likely to be destroyed by high temperatures. They are made in the same way but with cold water, and left to infuse for up to 12 hours. Herbs that need to be made up in this way include those containing a high proportion of mucilage, such as comfrey and marshmallow.

Preparing a decoction

Herbs with hard woody textures have tough cell walls, which need greater heat to break them down before they can release their constituents into the water. Nuts, seeds, bark, wood, roots and rhizomes are all made into decoctions. First they are broken up into small pieces, perhaps even powdered, so that they can be more easily absorbed by the water.

Using the same proportions of water and herbs as for infusions, the herbs are placed in a saucepan and covered with water. The saucepan should preferably be enamelled and definitely not aluminium, as some of the constituents of the plants interact chemically with this metal. Cover the saucepan, bring the water to the boil and simmer gently for 10-15 minutes, then strain and drink hot, unless otherwise specified.

Syrups

A sugar and water solution can be added to tinctures, and sugar can be added to infusions, to make syrups. Syrups are wonderful for children or when used to mask the taste of bitter herbs.

Pour 600ml/1 pint boiling water over 1.25kg/2½lb sugar and stir over a gentle heat until the sugar dissolves and the solution reaches the boil. One part of the tincture can be mixed with three parts syrup, and will keep indefinitely.

To sweeten an infusion, mix 350g/12oz sugar into 600ml/1 pint of infusion and heat until the sugar has dissolved. Keep in a cool place — preferably in the fridge.

Tablets and capsules

Occasionally it is useful to give remedies in tablet or capsule form. The practitioner usually buys these from large suppliers, but dedicated herbalists can make them up themselves by using powdered herbs. Gelatine capsules can easily be filled with a mixture of the appropriate herbs, and there are special gadgets for making hundreds at a time.

However, there are certain herbs which should not be given in capsules, notably those with a bitter taste. It is important to taste the bitterness in order to obtain maximum therapeutic value from the remedy, as this by reflex affects other functions in the rest of the alimentary tract.

EXTERNAL REMEDIES

There are many constituents in herbs which are readily absorbed through the skin, a fact that aromatherapists have been able to use to great advantage.

Herbal baths

A very pleasant, even luxurious way to take herbal medicine is in the form of a lovely warm bath. You can place a muslin bag with fresh aromatic herbs under the hot tap, or add a couple of drops of an aromatic oil or a pint (600ml) of herbal infusion to the bath and soak in it.

Herbal baths are an ancient form of treatment, and in many more primitive cultures they are still respected as a valid type of therapy. They should be warm, not too hot, and they used to be taken in a special oak tub, for 10-30 minutes. Handfuls of the herbs would be put directly into the bathwater, although this is not a good idea nowadays as they tend to clog up the plumbing system! They are best wrapped first in muslin bags.

The volatile oils from the herbs are absorbed not only through the pores of the skin, which are opened up by the warm water, but also through the nose and lungs in the inhalation of steam. The oils carried on the steam pass from the lungs directly into the blood stream, and messages are sent to the brain from the nose via nerve receptors. Thus the oils are assimilated directly and rapidly, which makes this a particularly suitable treatment for relaxing and soothing the nervous system.

So a wonderfully fragrant bath of perhaps lavender, rosemary or lemon balm can also be an effective medium for treatment. A chamomile bath is very useful for irritable children at the end of the day. It quietens them, soothes away irritability and encourages an easy and restful sleep. Limeflower baths are still used in France to help children to sleep. Mustard foot baths are an old British remedy for all the afflictions of our climate from colds to arthritis.

The French expert in this kind of treatment is the famous herbalist Maurice Mességué. He has made popular tradition of hand and foot bath therapy passed down from generations of country people in the Gers region of France where he grew up. He has written books about it, and describes how his patients have been cured simply by taking herbal foot baths for eight minutes in the evening and hand baths for the same time in the morning. The hands and feet are particularly sensitive areas where the active constituents of the plants can pass directly into the body through the skin, bypassing the rigours of the digestive tract.

As with infusions and decoctions, the only drawback

with this method of administration is that it takes a little time and trouble to prepare, and so it will only be adopted by patients who are especially interested in their own welfare — or who don't like taking medicine! It is an excellent way of treating children and babies who are too young or don't want to take medicines orally.

Other external treatments

Ointments may be given, especially for skin problems, varicose veins or internal problems such as rheumatism and arthritis. They can either be commercially prepared and bought in by the practitioner, or made up on the premises.

Any herb, fresh or dried, can be used to make an ointment. A very simple way to prepare an ointment involves macerating 350g/12oz of the herb in a mixture of

450g/1lb pure olive oil and 50g/2oz beeswax for a few hours over a low heat in a bain-marie or double saucepan over simmering water. Once the active constituents of the plant have been absorbed by the oil, the mixture can be pressed out and the herb discarded. The oil then cools and solidifies into an ointment.

Creams can be made simply by using aqueous cream from the chemist as a base and stirring in the herb in the form of a tincture, infusion or decoction. A few drops of essential oil can be used instead.

Compresses

Hot or cold compresses are recommended for a bad headache, a swollen arthritic joint, abdominal colic or period pains. A clean cloth is soaked in a decoction or

CABBAGE LEAF POULTICES ARE EXCELLENT FOR PAINFUL ARTHRITIC JOINTS

infusion of the herb and applied repeatedly to the affected area.

Poultices
These are like compresses but involved the use of the plant itself, rather than an infusion or decoction.

Place the fresh or dried herb between two layers of thin gauze. If you are using fresh herbs, bruise the leaves, stems or roots first. Add a little hot water to dried herbs to make a paste. The poultice can then be bound to the afflicted area with a light cotton bandage and kept warm with a hot water bottle. Cabbage poultices are excellent for painful arthritic joints, and a bran poultice is wonderful for relieving mastitis.

Liniments
A rubbing oil or liniment can be used in massage to relax or stimulate muscles and ligaments, or to soothe away pain. Liniments usually consist of a mixture of herbal oils and alcoholic tinctures of the herb required, and are intended to be absorbed rapidly by the skin. For this reason they often contain stimulating essential oils or capsicum.

Suppositories
Herbal suppositories and douches may also be prescribed. The former are for rectal or vaginal absorption, and the latter for vaginal insertion, enabling local problems to be treated quickly and directly.

The simplest way to make a suppository is to add the dried herb, which has been finely powdered, to a base of melted cocoa butter. Use this to fill a small mould made from aluminium foil. Let it cool and store in the fridge.

Oils
The essential oils used by aromatherapists and herbalists are pure oils, extracted from aromatic plants such as thyme, rosemary, lavender and peppermint by a process of distillation. Because the method of extraction is

complicated, they are obtained through suppliers and not made up at the practice.

Herbal oils by contrast can be prepared more simply. Finely chopped herbs are infused in a glass jar of pure vegetable oil such as olive, sunflower, or almond oil, placed in a sunny spot for two to three weeks and shaken daily. After that, the oil can be filtered off the plant and stored in a dark container. St John's wort flowers can be used in this fashion, and produce a wonderful red oil known as 'heart of Jesus oil', which is used as a healing agent for cuts and sores, and painful conditions of the nerves, such as trigeminal neuralgia and shingles.

HERBS IN FOOD

The most obvious way to take herbs is of course to eat them. No doubt this was the first way in which herbs were used by our ancestors. Certain herbs can be added to salads — dandelions and sorrel leaves, mint and lemon balm, marigold and borage flowers.

All the well-known culinary herbs exert a mild medicinal action, and while they impart an excellent flavour to our food, perhaps their original purpose was medicinal rather than culinary. It is interesting that most of the culinary herbs have antiseptic action, especially useful in the days before fridges! Lemon juice, another antiseptic, tastes good with fish, and has the added benefit of dissolving the bones should they inadvertently become lodged in the throat.

THE ACTUAL PRESCRIPTION

At the end of the first consultation, the herbalist will make out a prescription for medicine which is designed to suit the needs of the individual as far as possible. Human beings are so complex that no two people are ever the same and so no two medicines are either; each one is tailor-made.

'Simples' and 'Mixtures'

Some herbalists advocate the use of 'simples', where a sole herb is chosen for its variety of different actions. Take celery seed for example, which is used daily in herbal practices for arthritis, gout and rheumatism. It helps to eliminate acid wastes from the body by combining with them and hastening their removal from the tissues. It also acts on the kidneys to aid production of urine (i.e. it is a diuretic) and so facilitates cleansing in that way. It has the effect of elevating mood, lifting depression and toning the nervous system. It allays underlying stresses and tensions, which encourages the patient to cope better and hence aids recovery.

Other herbalists advocate the use of 'mixtures', and may compose a prescription containing anything between five and 20 different herbs. Many herbs are considered best used in combination as they each enhance the action of the other and thereby work 'synergistically'.

Synergism

Synergism is the interaction of different agents, such that the total effect is greater than the sum of the parts. It occurs between many different herbs. For example, lobelia and capsicum work excellently together, acting on the lungs and circulation. Daucus (wild carrot) and alchemilla (lady's mantle) are useful together for kidney stones and gravel. Synergism also occurs between ingredients of the same herb.

The prescription of many remedies together multiplies the synergistic effects of the herbs, and a skilful herbalist will know how to use this to advantage. Synergism can help to direct the remedy to a particular area or system of the body. It obviously enhances the power of the medicine and triggers mechanisms of self-regulation in the body, which means that dosages of the remedies can be kept to a minimum.

An example

If we return (see page 69) to the girl with the skin problem acne, who also had hormonal imbalance, we can illustrate these ideas a little. By talking to her I learned that she experienced quite a bit of flatulence and bloating after eating. She was also having trouble in her relationship with her boyfriend. I prescribed a remedy containing several different herbs, some of which would help to clear the skin by their action on the liver (yellow dock root, barberry bark, burdock, fumitory) or on the lymphatic system (clivers, poke root). The liver herbs would remedy the digestive problems, relieving the flatulence and discomfort.

The anxiety associated with her boyfriend was clearly affecting her health. To support the overworked nervous system I prescribed chamomile, vervain or red clover flowers, which also act on the skin and gastro-intestinal tract. Other tonics such as skullcap borage or wild oats would also be useful.

... LIVER HERBS SUCH AS BURDOCK WOULD REMEDY DIGESTIVE PROBLEMS, RELIEVING FLATULENCE AND DISCOMFORT...

The hormonal imbalance related to her period problems could be sorted out simply by using *Vitex agnus* cactus, or false unicorn flower. The addition of a little capsicum to enhance the action of the herbs and stimulate the circulation would enable the remedial constituents of the plants to be carried to the areas of the body requiring them.

THE PRESCRIPTION

Each bottle of prescribed medicine carries a label describing how it should be taken. The dosage is usually a teaspoonful taken three times daily. This is halved for · children and old people, but can be doubled in acute cases. Sometimes only a few drops are required to be taken regularly through the day.

Herbs are best taken either before or after a meal, but this is not essential. If the patient does not eat three meals a day or is fasting or on a restricted diet, or forgets to take the dose at the right time, it is nevertheless important to continue taking the medicine as regularly as possible, either with a drink or on its own.

The medicine is usually best taken in hot water, but cold water may be used. The quantity of water is not really important. You may be given a small dispensing measure to ensure the right dosage, and this can be topped up with water, or added to a wineglassful of water.

While taking any herbal medicine, it is best to avoid conventional medicine for minor problems that may crop up. Antibiotics will suppress an infection, but they also suppress the vital energy of the patient which the herbs are attempting to improve. So orthodox medicine will negate much of the purpose of the herbs and should be taken only when really necessary. If minor problems arise, they are best discussed with your herbalist who will advise or prescribe accordingly.

If your condition changes or you have any queries while taking herbal medicine, it us advisable to contact your herbalist rather than wait until the next appointment. Sometimes, at the onset of treatment, a patient can experience a brief exacerbation of the symptoms, or develop a cold or some other mild acute illness. This is known as a 'healing crisis'. It is the result of the energy which has been generated by the herbal remedy to help fight off illness. Symptoms reflect the power of the vital force: chronic symptoms indicate diminished energy, while acute symptoms represent a short concentrated effort to cleanse the system. Thus the healing crisis is nature's way of clearing out accumulated waste products. Your herbalist will advise you on the best way to deal with this, should it arise.

HOLD YOUR NOSE AND OPEN YOUR MOUTH !

6.
THE EFFECTS OF HERBAL TREATMENT

THE SECOND VISIT

At the end of the initial consultation the patient usually goes home with a bottle of medicine or other 'lotions and potions' that may have been prescribed, a diet sheet and sometimes directions for certain remedial exercises. An appointment card will show the date of the patient's next visit.

The course of the second visit depends very much on how the first consultation developed. If there was a long and complex medical history, the time allotted may have been taken up entirely with physical details. Alternatively, the patient's problems may have emerged more on an emotional level. In either case, missing gaps in the case history can then be filled in.

The return visit also allows the herbalist to make sure that the patient is on the right track with the treatment, that the medicine is suitable and its administration presents no difficulties, and that dietary advice has been fully understood and followed. Any problems concerning changes in eating habits or lifestyle can be discussed and ironed out. People who have been accustomed for decades to eating in an unhealthy fashion may experience a few difficulties in adjusting, but once they get over the first few hurdles it is usually plain sailing. Often patients are quite excited by the process, and they may come armed with lists of questions the herbalist is only to happy to answer.

A patient who was tense and anxious, and held back considerably during the initial discussion, may find that the ice breaks a little during the second visit and that more of the story unfolds. In some cases the practitioner only discovers the root of the patient's ill-health on the fourth or fifth visit; in others, patient and practitioner may spark something off in each other on first meeting that enables free communication from the onset.

If you find it hard to talk about yourself, the person behind the physical symptoms, the herbalist may attempt to make it clear that your emotions, thoughts and spiritual life are as important to your health or illness as are the organs and cells of your body. A restoration to health may involve change on all levels, physical, emotional and mental, and the responsibility for this lies with the individual.

After all, it is not the herbalist but the patient who heals. The herbalist merely offers advice and prescribes herbs, which are used as a tool to stimulate the patient's own healing energy. The more the patient is able to reveal to the practitioner, the easier that process becomes. If the patient truly wants to recover, talking openly should present few problems. The patient is free to choose.

SUBSEQUENT VISITS

In most instances, at the close of the second visit a further appointment is arranged. How far ahead depends largely on the nature of the problem. If the patient has a chronic physical problem that is not likely to change rapidly, then the appointment could be made three to four weeks ahead. But if there is an acute or serious physical problem, or if the patient is emotionally or mentally troubled, it is probably more beneficial to meet within a week or two.

Someone with a physical condition such as back pain, rheumatism or muscular problems, or who is suffering from a great deal of stress and tension, may benefit from regular massage with herbal oils, in which case this can be arranged.

The system of appointments is designed to relate to the individual needs of each patient. There are financial considerations also, of course. The visits continue until the patient is well on the way to recovery, and both herbalist and patient are satisfied that no more appointments are necessary.

If the treatment is going to be long-term, as is often the case with chronic illness, appointments may be made every three or even six months, and medicine will continue to be taken in between.

HOW LONG WILL THE TREATMENT TAKE TO WORK?

The process of recovery using herbal remedies involves a three-way interplay among the practitioner, the herbal medicine and the patient.

It is easy to recognize the healer in those patients who are already quite determined to get well. They nearly always succeed — we are all aware of how people have conquered cancer and other serious illnesses through their will to live. We may also be aware that there are many people who are not ready or who do not really wish to get well, and in these cases the treatment is not to blame if they fail to recover at the rate expected. Healing must come from within.

It would be safe to say that the harder you work at getting well, the more easily you recover. It is important to put into operation all the therapeutic measures the practitioner suggests. The herbalist does most of the initial work in assessing the nature of the patient's condition, and recommending and prescribing certain treatments. But from then on it is up to the individual efforts of the patient. The practitioner acts almost as a guide, with the patient returning every now and then for an up-to-date assessment of progress.

The appointments system functions almost as a necessary disciplinary measure, serving as an incentive for many people to try out and report back on the herbalist's suggestions. Once the treatment has proved itself beneficial the patient will be keen to adopt a more healthy lifestyle. Until then the herbalist offers support, and sometimes even acts as a confessor.

If you find it too difficult to stick to your diet, or you don't have the time to take exercise daily, or the enthusiasm to practise the recommended relaxation technique, or the courage to sort out difficulties in a close relationship, then you will probably find that the treatment will take longer to work. However, happily, there are always surprises. Some people seem to recover remarkably quickly with apparently little effort on their part, because their vitality is good.

A patient's psychological attitude has far-reaching effects in determining the length and effectiveness of the treatment. Many people feel attracted to herbal medicine through a love of flowers, plants and nature. Others may not have this affinity, indeed they may not like taking the herbs prescribed and feel resentful of the efforts they are required to make, and because of this they counteract the healing effect. These patients would perhaps respond better to other therapies — acupuncture, homoeopathy, chiropractic or spiritual healing.

Patients sometimes have unconscious ulterior motives for perpetuating ill-health. Someone who has been ill for many years and sought treatment far and wide before finally landing up on the herbalist's doorstep, could actually be using the illness as a psychological prop. A patient like this may be seeking attention as a substitute for love and a fulfilling relationship, or may fear facing up to life's responsibilities — illness provides an excellent and permanent excuse. Should the practitioner confront the patient with this idea, the patient can either ignore the facts or take responsibility for them and begin to change.

The length of the treatment is also closely related to the development of the relationship between the practitioner and the patient. In many cases this relationship has already started long before the first consultation. It may have begun when the patient first heard friends or neighbours discussing their own experiences with the herbalist. Often the patient has great confidence in the herbalist and in herbal remedies before even setting eyes on the practitioner. This helps treatment tremendously.

I have often found that the farther away the patient lives and the more effort is required to see the herbalist, the quicker that person recovers. The herbalist must have been very highly recommended to inspire the patient to make a long journey instead of consulting someone else more local. The confidence in the practitioner has already started to have its effect before the treatment has even begun. This is called the 'placebo effect'. The incentive to recover quickly can also be greater if the visits to the herbalist disrupt the patient's lifestyle. A long journey may mean missing a day's work. However, equally, the incentive to recover may be lacking altogether if the patient has been persuaded to visit the herbalist against his or her wishes.

It is not possible for the same practitioner to appeal to every patient. Some people prefer a woman, others a man; some look for a young, go-ahead and up-to-date practitioner, others feel more comfortable with somebody older and more experienced. Some will feel an immediate

THE FURTHER AWAY THE PERSON LIVES AND THE MORE EFFORT IS REQUIRED TO SEE THE HERBALIST, THE QUICKER THE PERSON RECOVERS!

Actually, I'm looking for Bryce the herbalist, but it doesn't matter now because I'm feeling better anyway...

trust and liking for the practitioner and appreciate the care and understanding they receive, while others may never be able to get over the idea that, to them, herbal medicine smacks of 'witchcraft'. Recovery also depends on the general health and vitality of the patient.

Some people approach a herbalist only once their physical condition has deteriorated to such a point that organic change has developed and cannot be reversed. It is not possible to work miracles with incurable conditions, which may include Parkinson's disease, multiple sclerosis, severe osteo- and rheumatoid arthritis, and ankylosing spondylitis. If these problems could have been treated at the onset, then the vitality of the patient, the energy of the vital force, would have been less depleted and the potential for healing far greater.

However, in these instances there is still much positive work that patients can do. The herbs, a change of diet, and a re-evaluation of their lifestyle, will almost definitely raise their general level of health and vitality, and they will be much better equipped to cope with their physical condition. Small associated functional problems may disappear and much of the pain and discomfort experienced in a condition such as arthritis can be relieved. Inflammatory processes can be halted; but nothing can, for example, alter or reverse the ulnar deviation of a rheumatoid arthritis sufferer, once the tissues have altered structurally.

Herbal medicine is always effective at some level of human experience. A patient taking herbal remedies may still have the 'pill rolling' tremor of Parkinson's disease, but could feel much better mentally and emotionally, freed from the anxiety, depression, lethargy and fear that used to accompany the physical state. The vital energy of the patient, once re-emerged, could provide strength to deal with the physical symptoms, which may even appear less significant, and energy would thus be available to direct to other aspects of the patient's life — including the spiritual.

If consulting a medical herbalist means that the patient begins to look at the significance of the illness, and assess the deeper causes of the physical problem, it must be a positive thing. If it means a dramatic improvement in the patient's lifestyle and a resulting sense of well-being, herbal medicine can undoubtedly be said to be effective.

As far as the remedy itself is concerned, the long history of herbalism going back to the dawn of civilization is certainly proof enough that herbal medicines work. Had they not worked, they would have been discarded long ago. When herbs are properly prescribed and taken for long enough, they are always effective to some degree, as they enhance the action of the vital force which is always seeking to restore health, balance and harmony.

Today more and more plants are proving their age-old medicinal virtues under scientific scrutiny. The latest is feverfew, for which official clinical trials have recently been approved. A pharmacologist working with this herb found that seven out of ten migraine sufferers being treated with the plant claimed that their attacks had disappeared or become less frequent. The plant's medicinal qualities have long been known, however. In 1772, a herbalist wrote: 'In the worst headaches, this herb exceeds whatever else is known.'

In mild acute problems — aches and pains, sore throats, stomach-aches, burns and cuts — herbs can act as quickly as any modern orthodox medicines. When treating long-standing chronic illness, such as bronchitis or arthritis, the herbs work gently and slowly and have a cumulative action, strengthening the body generally and improving the function of the various systems and organs over a fairly lengthy period of time — weeks, months or sometimes years, depending on the vitality of the patient.

Usually the length and effectiveness of treatment depends on the following factors:

1 The severity of the condition.
2 How long the person has been ill — as a general rule, however many years one has been ill, it takes as many months to recover.
3 The age and vitality of the patient, including

SEVEN OUT OF TEN PEOPLE USING FEVERFEW FOUND THAT
THEIR MIGRAINE ATTACKS WERE GONE OR WERE LESS FREQUENT,

hereditary factors. Children will generally recover
quickly. The younger the patient, the more vitality
there should be.

4 The complications arising as a result of drug therapy
– so-called iatrogenic disease.

5 How much effort the patient puts into the treatment
and how much the patient works against it — one
cannot expect herbal medicine to produce good
results in the long term when people continue to
undermine their vitality with poor diet, too little fresh
air and exercise, and a high level of stress and
tension.

6 The psychological attitude of the patient — whether
he or she actually wants to get better.

7 The relationship between the patient and the
practitioner.

Herbal treatment is basically a matter of letting nature take its course and allowing the inherent wisdom of the healing force to determine the appropriate length of the treatment — we should not impede our progress with too much impatience.

WHAT BENEFITS CAN BE EXPECTED?

At the start of herbal treatment and with amended diet and lifestyle, the healing energies within the patient begin to change. For many the action of the vital force may have been suppressed and depleted for months or years. When the habits contributing to this suppression, such as poor diet, lack of fresh air, negative thinking and the many other factors, suddenly change, a weight is taken off the patient, and the vital energy has the opportunity to reassert itself.

Since symptoms reflect the efforts of the vital force to protect itself and to ward off illness, when this power starts to increase then for a short period the symptoms can increase accordingly. This is the 'healing crisis' discussed in Chapter 5.

For many people, however, there is no such healing crisis and the recovery begins gently and gradually. In the two weeks that normally elapse between the first and second visits, most patients with chronic problems may not necessarily see a diminishing of their symptoms, but they tend to feel generally better in themselves. Over the next few weeks there should be a gradual but appreciable change and improvement.

Even if herbal remedies are used in the relatively short term, perhaps for an acute problem, or a mild chronic complaint such as rhinitis or eczema, they ensure better health in the long run. Since the condition has not been suppressed by other inappropriate forms of treatment, which lead to further accumulation of toxins and depletion of vital energy, and the body has been aided in its cleansing process, the patient should actually feel much better after the treatment than before falling ill.

If the patient manages to approach the real underlying causes of the illness, and seeks to remedy them with the help of herbal medicine, this can mean a great turnaround towards good health. If the illness in its true sense is ignored, if it is suppressed and the causes pushed under the carpet, it will simply recur at a later time in a similar way or in a more serious form. If the cause is recognized, there is a fresh opportunity to experience wholeness and a wonderful sense of well-being on all levels.

Once the initial effort has been made, the changes in health and lifestyle that come about through herbal treatment can easily be incorporated into daily life. This is the preventive medicine of the future, for it enables us to maintain homoeostasis, despite the variables affecting our inner and outer lives, for a greater length of time.

The physiological action of the herbs on the body after a period of treatment should leave all parts of the body in better condition. Tone, vigour and function are restored to over-stressed and over-relaxed parts of the body. The nervous system, hormonal balance and circulation will also benefit from the regulatory action of the herbs. Nutrition of all the cells and tissues will be improved, and the elimination of waste products facilitated.

IS HERBAL MEDICINE TOTALLY SAFE?

While modern medicines are subject to a wide variety of tests on animals to prove their safety, and still result in a range of side-effects, herbs have already proved their safety and efficacy through thousands of years of use. Herbal remedies have stood the test of time, while many drugs have not. Drugs are frequently withdrawn from the market after causing death, handicap or deformity, and iatrogenic disease (caused by drug treatment) forms a large branch of medical practice. There is no record of this occurring through the use of prescribed doses of herbal medicine. Tests that are harmful to animals have no place in herbal medicine.

Most herbal medicines are perfectly safe and mild.

However, it would be a mistake to assume that, because herbal medicine is safe and free from side-effects when used with care in experienced hands, any number of herbal remedies can be swallowed with impunity. They can certainly be abused if taken in excess like any other food or drink. In one well-known case, a man died from drinking excessive quantities of carrot juice.

Is it safe for children?

Herbs can certainly be taken at any age, and are infinitely preferable to the powerful and sometimes dangerous medicines like cortisone and antihistamines which are frequently doled out to even the youngest of children.

Mild herbal infusions to drink, herbs added to the bath, hand and foot baths, and massages with herbal oils, are wonderful ways to treat children. In many ways the herbs are more effective in bringing swift relief for minor problems. Raspberry vinegar and sage can be used for sore throats instead of antibiotics. Colic in babies and children can easily be remedied with fennel, mint or chamomile. Headaches can be taken away with peppermint compresses, and proprietary pain-killing drugs can be thrown in the bin. Chamomile, lemon balm and limeflower will ensure a good night's sleep, comfrey and calendula can be used for diaper rash, and peppermint, yarrow and elderflowers in a hot tea can treat colds, flu and fevers in record time.

If children are happy, with a good diet, plenty of fresh air and exercise, they have every chance of being healthy. If they should get ill, they need only the mildest of medicines and plenty of rest to recover completely in no time at all. If every time they get a cold or cough, throat infection or tummy bug they are given powerful and inappropriate medicines, their vital energy will soon dwindle, as will their natural resistance. If children are treated with gentle herbs for the simple childhood ailments that tend to be self-limiting anyway, they should respond to small doses of herbal remedies or other medicines if ever they become seriously ill in the future.

HEADACHES CAN BE TAKEN AWAY BY PEPPERMINT COMPRESSES, AND PROPRIETARY DRUGS CAN BE THROWN OUT THE WINDOW.

Is it safe to take herbal medicine and medicine from the doctor?

Generally speaking it is quite safe to combine herbal and conventional medicines. But many people consult a herbalist because the medicines they have been prescribed are not working. In this case, once herbal remedies are being taken, the others can be left off as there is no point in taking both. Others go to a herbalist because although the drugs they are taking may be controlling their illness, they are suffering unpleasant side-effects and are looking for a natural alternative. In these cases, the patient would probably take both drugs and herbs together for a while, and then gradually and with careful monitoring decrease the drugs.

It is not always a good idea to abandon medicines from the doctor immediately at the start of herbal treatment. Often there can be unpleasant withdrawal symptoms, such as when stopping tranquilizers and cortisone. It is most important to tell your herbalist about any drugs you may be taking. There are certain drugs that need close monitoring, notably anti-coagulants, insulin for diabetes, and drugs for anxiety and depression.

If the patient is taking any of these, it would be preferable for the herbalist and doctor to confer, with the patient's permission of course. Sometimes patients beginning treatment are uneasy about discussing their visit to a herbalist with the doctor, in case they meet with disapproval. Once well on the road to recovery, most tend to feel more confident about broaching the subject.

7.
HERBAL
MEDICINE AND
THE LAW

HISTORICAL BACKGROUND

Herbalists have never been consulted when laws have been made concerning the use of herbs, with the result that legislation tends to restrict herbalism rather than support it. Some herbs have even been in danger of disappearing completely because their use has been forbidden to the herbal practitioner, and granted only to orthodox doctors who usually have no interest in the subject.

Today, herbal medicine operates under the same guidelines as conventional medicine, guidelines which were drawn up in the wake of the thalidomide tragedy. They are:

1 To guarantee the safety of the public when using medicines.

2 To standardize plant remedies with proper botanical identification and quality control.

3 To produce sufficient evidence of the therapeutic ability of the medicine.

Naturally the herbal profession welcomes any scientific inquiry if it increases our knowledge about the herbs we use in daily practice. However, we consider that herbs are in danger because herbalists are not represented on any of the decision-making bodies. All official enquiries into herbs have been carried out by people with an orthodox scientific viewpoint, i.e. doctors, chemists and pharmacists.

It is also worth remembering that herbal remedies have been proved in use over thousands of years, and have never been implicated in any disaster such as thalidomide.

HERBS UNDER ATTACK

Herbs are under attack mainly because those investigating them do not acknowledge or appreciate the difference between the action of the whole plant and that of a single active substance extracted from it. If one tiny substance among the many contained in the plant shows any sign of toxicity, or even pharmacological activity when fed to or injected in huge amounts into susceptible experimental animals, the whole plant is likely to be scheduled as a 'prescription only' herb, for use by doctors and not by herbalists. This means doom to the herb concerned since doctors are only interested in prescribing the extract, and never the whole plant.

If the same criteria used for herbs were applied to drugs, most synthetic drugs would be withdrawn and many pharmacists' shelves would stand empty. And, as Fred Fletcher-Hyde says, if these criteria were applied to the vegetable kingdom, it would result in lettuce, radish, watercress, tomatoes, horseradish, mustard and-cress and

111

celery all disappearing from the greengrocer's, for they all demonstrate pharmacological activity, as do spinach, rhubarb, asparagus, onions, leeks, potatoes, beans, parsnips and carrots. Plums, cherries, nectarines, apricots and pears all contain cyanogenetic glycosides and, along with bananas, would be available on prescription only.

Many campaigns against specific herbs have already been successful. Rauwolfia, mentioned in Chapter 1 as a treatment for 'moon madness', is forbidden for use by herbalists. From the herbalist's point of view this is the result of sheer prejudice and refusal to accept the findings of real scientific observation.

Comfrey has been blamed for being toxic to the liver because of the pyrrolizidine alkaloids it contains, and has been reported to cause liver tumours when injected in large amounts into rats.

Liquorice, used for indigestion and peptic ulcers, has been said to cause retention of sodium and loss of potassium and so encourage the onset of high blood pressure and severe hypokalaemia (loss of blood potassium).

Pennyroyal has also been incriminated. The oil extracted from this herb is a traditional abortifacient. Two cases have been reported where it causes severe liver damage used in this way — one patient died.

IN DEFENCE

Comfrey has been eaten or made into a tea for centuries, during which time there has been no single instance of toxic effects ever recorded following its use.

The case against comfrey is based on two misconceptions. First, that the other naturally occurring substances in the whole comfrey plant have no action themselves, serving simply to dilute the alkaloids. In fact the mucilage and allantoin contained in comfrey has made it famous as a wonderfully soothing remedy for healing all types of connective tissue, including bone and cartilage. Second, that the human metabolism is identical to that of a rat, which is susceptible to large amounts of these alkaloids, and not to that of a sheep, which is resistant to them.

On the basis of these assumptions and without any actual evidence against the safety of comfrey, its use is likely to be forbidden in the near future. This seems ridiculous, as tea, almonds, apples, pears, mustard, radishes and hops, to name but a few, all contain substances which, if they were to be extracted and tested under similar conditions to those used in comfrey experiments, would be shown to be poisonous. It seems unlikely that we could ever be forced to ignore our experience of the use and wholesomeness of these foods and ban their sale because no scientific evidence has been published to prove their safety. Yet this is exactly what is happening to comfrey.

One of the few investigations into comfrey has shown that extracts of the whole plant restrict the growth of cancerous tumours in mice.

Liquorice: All cases of adverse reactions to this herb are quoted by Martindale (an authoritative guide to medicines) to have affected only those people who are addicted to liquorice sweets and ingest large amounts of them regularly over a long period of time. Should each packet of candy carry a government health warning?

Pennyroyal: The people who suffered from liver damage and died (see opposite) were not, it is important to note, taking the herb, but a highly concentrated oil extracted from it. Pennyroyal tea contains very little of the oil and is perfectly safe (though not recommended in pregnancy). It would be necessary to drink 75 gallons of strong tea from the herb to obtain the same effect as 25g/ 1oz (the fatal dose) of the oil.

There is a growing list of threatened herbs, including St John's wort, coltsfoot, sweet flag, wormwood and even ginseng. While increasing attention is being paid to herbal medicine by the public and the media, the medical press continues its opposition. Naturally herbalists need to

THE ONLY ADVERSE REACTIONS TO LIQUORICE OCCUR
THROUGH EATING TOO MANY LIQUORICE SWEETS .

be aware of new findings about herbal remedies, but if the
doubts about their safety or efficacy are based only on
testing massive doses of single extracted constituents of
the plant on laboratory animals, we would certainly be
wise to ignore them.

It might be more expedient for orthodox science to turn
its critical eye on itself and look at the drug industry. It is
not easy to forget the thalidomide tragedy back in the
1960s. The drug was a sedative offered to expectant
mothers for morning sickness and its supposed safety was
its selling point. In 1961 an advertisement in a medical
journal called it 'outstandingly safe'. But a few days later
a report was published linking it to foetal abnormalities
and the drug was withdrawn. Sadly, there was so little

publicity about this that many women had no idea of the risks and continued taking it for some time, with devastating results.

Despite the legal restrictions, many drugs are prescribed while still in experimental stages, or marketed after incomplete trials. Financial gain may be largely responsible for this. The drug companies can well afford to court doctors, and major drug firms often sponsor conferences and other gatherings in exotic locations.

Many terrible drug side-effects are never reported, and even where there are doubts about the safety of drugs, still they are not withdrawn. In their book *Cured to Death – the effect of prescription drugs*, Melville and Johnson reveal that over one million people every year suffer an adverse drug reaction. They say that in minor ailments the side-effects to the drug may be worse than the original complaint. And yet the innocent herb remains a target for attack.

Many in the orthodox medical world advocate that herbal medicines should be supplied only through pharmacies, where qualified people can be relied upon to advise the public about the efficacy and possible side-effects of the different herbs. They claim that there is no sound evidence to support the safety and efficacy of most herbal medicines. Yet how much does this have to do with public interest, and how much with the perceived financial benefits? Are not the pharmacists and others just jumping on the bandwagon?

RESEARCH INTO HERBAL MEDICINE

A medical magazine for doctors offered a pull-out supplement on the efficacy and safety of herbal remedies, designed to help answer patients' queries about preparations available at health food shops.

The author (Dr William Count) admitted that most pharmaceutical research into the plant world had consisted in the past of frank exploitation of plants as sources for new compounds, or foundations on which to synthesize allopathic medicines. He rightly stated that what is required when researching herbal remedies is 'a much broader picture of the total chemistry of the herbal plant', that is, one should look at the whole plant. He called for scientists carrying out clinical trials to bear in mind the holistic philosophy of herbal medicine. Happily there *is* some support for the herbal view among the orthodox.

Clearly modern research techniques have much to offer in the assessment and validation of traditional herbal remedies. But for the busy herbal practitioner the problems of undertaking research are enormous, in respect of both time and money. Herbalists do not have access to the vast funds commanded by the drug companies, for no profit is likely.

Then there is the question of how to approach such research. Our ethical code disapproves of experiments on animals, and is opposed to the use of double blind trials, which deprive many of those involved of access to herbal treatment, and are also impractical owing to the highly individualistic prescription requirements for each patient.

Some progress in research has, however, been made. Much information relating to herbal medicines has been collated and codified, and standard reference works on botanical medicines have now been published.

Research material from all over the world has been collected and stored on a central computer. Research has been started to validate the efficacy of plant medicine. Clinical records of patients seen in practice are being collated to assess the therapeutic effects of the herbs and any side-effects.

Bridges are being built between orthodox and complementary medicine, as public confidence in holistic medicine grows. A considerable amount of research is also being carried out abroad, particularly in France and Germany, where there is great interest in herbal medicine from within the medical profession.

FUTURE PROSPECTS

It is estimated that four million people a year use some form of complementary medicine, not counting the thousands of people who go to faith healers or treat themselves at home.

Leading practitioners of the main alternative therapies – acupuncture, herbal medicine, homoeopathy, osteopathy and chiropractic – have been grouping together with a view to protecting themselves and the general public against restrictive legislation. In addition, it appears that not all doctors are prejudiced against alternative medicine. One study showed that approximately two-thirds of family doctors in training showed interest in learning at least one alternative therapy, and a third said that they already referred patients to alternative practitioners. Increasing interest in alternative medicine is encouraging doctors to give this approach to health a chance, or at least to keep an open mind.

Despite the repeated attacks on herbal remedies in the media and the medical press, and the serious restrictions in the use of some very valuable herbs, herbal medicine is gaining in popularity. In the long term, only public support can ensure its survival. The use of herbal medicine for worldwide health care has also been backed by the World Health Organization. In 1976 it issued a report strongly promoting the use of traditional medicine in developing nations.

The scope for herbal medicine is enormous. Of the 400,000 species of higher plants on earth, only 10 per cent have ever been investigated. Herbal medicine can offer a less costly yet effective alternative treatment for many chronic problems seen in everyday practice. Orthodox medical resources are stretched to their limits in many parts of the world, and government cutbacks mean that lives are being lost unnecessarily.

Perhaps the history of medicine in the Western world will eventually turn full circle, and as unbiased scientific research unfolds and confirms more of the wonders of the plant world, we may find that herbal remedies have a more dramatic effect on health care than our ancestors ever dreamed of.

FURTHER
READING

The Illustrated Herbal Handbook, Juliette de Bairacli
Levy (Faber & Faber)
This is a fascinating book, with much useful and
practical information on the use of herbs, enriched by the
author's travels in many parts of the world and her
experiences with many wandering tribespeople. Added to
this, she is not only a writer, but also a botanist, farmer,
free physician, herb collector and herbalist.

Healing Plants, William Thomson (Macmillan)
A beautifully illustrated and practical herbal with full
descriptions of 240 different plants, plenty of information
on growing, harvesting and preserving them, instructions
for their use as well as a section on specific illnesses and
how to treat them with medicinal herbs.

The Way of Herbs, Michael Tierra (Unity Press, Santa
Cruz, USA)
A very informative book by a practising herbalist who has
a background of experience with the traditional healers of
China, India and America. Includes an excellent section on
the healing properties of herbs and their applications, and
a wide range of herbal recipes for treating many common
problems.

The Practice of Aromatherapy, Dr Jean Valnet (C.W. Daniel)
Written by one of the most important figures in the world of aromatherapy, this is the most detailed work (recently translated) in English on the use of essential oils. The book studies around 50 plants and essences, looking at their history, their properties, their use and administration. There is also a useful section on case histories.

The Medical Discoveries of Edward Bach, Physician, Nora Weeks (C.W. Daniel)
Dr Bach practised as a doctor for about 20 years including some time in Harley Street. He abandoned his practice in search of remedies to treat what we saw to be the real roots of illness — our emotional, mental and spiritual attitudes. This book describes Dr Bach's discoveries of the essences of wild flowers to treat problems such as fear, shock, depression and anxiety.

Holistic Herbal, David Hoffman (Findhorn Press)
Written by a practising medical herbalist this book presents an inspiringly holistic approach to herbal medicine, relating it not only to ourselves but also to the world around us. It describes the systems of the body and how herbs relate to them and their imbalances. It has informative sections on the chemistry of herbs and methods of preparation, herb-gathering and *materia medica*.

Green Pharmacy, Barbara Griggs (Norman & Hobhouse)
A wonderfully enlightening and detailed account of the history of herbalism — the events which have shaped the course of medicine and pharmacy and the rise and fall of herbal use from prehistoric times up to the present day.

School of Natural Healing, Dr J. Christopher (Biworld)
A reference book and a must for people seriously interested in studying herbal medicine in depth. It

provides a detailed guide to hundreds of herbs, with a
wealth of recipes for their practical application in a whole
range of ailments. However, there are a few mistakes.

Herbal Medicine, Dian Buchman (Gramercy)
Published in association with the Herb Society, the book
provides a detailed and practical guide to the use of herbs.
Excellent for the layperson.

A Modern Herbal, Mrs Grieve (Dover Publications)
Considered the most extensive and detailed 20th-century
herbal in English. It is recommended for all who have a
serious interest in herbal medicine, and includes
descriptions of each plant, the history of its use, the
constituents and medicinal actions as well as dosage.

Living Medicine, Mannfried Pahlow (Thorsons)
Written by a pharmacist and doctor, the book describes
those herbs whose efficacy has been acknowledged and
proved by science, while at the same time it presents an
interestingly holistic approach. Translated from German,
it provides a catalogue of herbs, their descriptions,
contents, use and preparation.

The Herb Book, John Lust (Bantam Books)
This American encyclopedia contains a wealth of
information on all aspects of herbal use, not simply medicinal.

Back to Eden, Jethro Kloss (Beneficial Books)
A classic book on herbal medicine and naturopathy,
originally published in 1939. Perhaps rather old-fashioned
now, but nevertheless interesting and informative.

Guide to Medicinal Plants, Schauenberg and Paris
(Lutterworth Press)
Originally published in French, this is basically a
reference book, with an interesting and extremely useful
presentation, grouping the medicinal herbs according to
their healing constituents.